Thorns in the Garden Planet

Vera C. Shaw

THOMAS NELSON PUBLISHERS
Nashville

Published in Nashville, Tennessee, by Thomas Nelson, Inc.

Scripture quotations noted J. B. PHILLIPS are from J. B. PHILLIPS: THE NEW TESTAMENT IN MODERN ENGLISH, Revised Edition. Copyright © J. B. Phillips 1958, 1960, 1972. Used by permission of Macmillan Publishing Co., Inc.

Scripture quotations noted NIV are taken from the HOLY BIBLE, NEW INTERNATIONAL VERSION ®. Copyright © 1973, 1978, 1984, by International Bible Society. Used by permission of Zondervan Bible Publishing House. All rights reserved.

The "NIV" and "New International Version" trademarks are registered in the United States Patent and Trademark Office by International Bible Society. Use of either trademark requires the permission of International Bible Society.

Scripture quotations noted NASB are from THE NEW AMERICAN STAN-DARD BIBLE, Copyright © 1960, 1962, 1963, 1968, 1971, 1972, 1973, 1975, 1977 by The Lockman Foundation and are used by permission.

Scripture quotations noted NEB are from THE NEW ENGLISH BIBLE. Copyright © 1961, 1970 by the Delegates of the Oxford University Press and the Syndics of the Cambridge University Press. Reprinted by permission.

Unless otherwise noted, Scripture quotations NKJV are from THE NEW KING JAMES VERSION. Copyright © 1979, 1980, 1982, Thomas Nelson, Inc., Publishers.

Library of Congress Cataloging-in-Publication Data

Shaw, Vera C.

Thorns in the garden planet : meditations on the Creator's care / Vera C. Shaw.

     p.   cm.

Includes bibliographical references.

ISBN 0-8407-7738-8

1. Human ecology—Religious aspects—Christianity—Meditations. 2. Creation—Meditations. 3. Gardens—Religious aspects—Christianity—Meditations. 4. Spiritual life—Christianity. I. Title.

BT695.5.S43   1993

261.8'362—dc20
                                 93-15678
                                      CIP

To Jim
who shares the meaning of it all

Contents

Foreword

Recently, eminent scientists, under the leadership of Dr. Carl Sagan, issued an appeal to religious leaders urging them to join with the scientific community in solving the environmental crisis. Many prominent Christian leaders—and indeed leaders of all faiths—individually and collectively, have been responding to this challenge. Even before the appeal was circulated, the Reverend Billy Graham was already on record: "We Christians," he said, "have a responsibility to take a lead in caring for the Earth."

It is very important, then, that a book should appear at this time, one deeply personal, yet at the same time one which draws upon Christian faith, to uncover and proclaim the profound relationship between faith and ecology. We need a book which declares unequivocally that we must turn to Christ if the human family is to solve its environmental crisis. The truth which we need to hear, especially today, is that Christ is the healer, the sustainer, and the renewer—not only of our individual souls, but also of all creation.

Such a book has come to us from Vera Shaw—*Thorns in the Garden Planet: Meditations on the Creator's Care.* A Christian evangelical active for many years in the Harvard-Radcliffe Christian Fellowship, Mrs. Shaw shares with her readers meditations that are an example for all of us who must write—at least in our hearts—our own, very personal, faith-inspired response to the environmental crisis that so threatens the creation which God calls good.

The meditations in *Thorns* are drawn from ancient biblical themes, yet presented amidst the crushing awareness of the devastation threatening the world's ecosystems. Quite unfashionably, Mrs. Shaw names the cause of our environmental woes: our human selfishness. She also trumpets the call of our environmental hope: the Risen Christ, the true gardener of the human soul, the true tender of the Father's creation.

A person from any religious tradition can read this book and find nourishment in this volume of reflections because Mrs. Shaw's faith is so deep that it touches the living waters of universal truth. Professing Christians will be especially drawn to its entwined themes for modern times: biblical Christianity and modern ecology. Today, to be a Christian is to be ecologically aware.

The book weaves reflections around three gardens— The Garden of Eden, where human selfishness erupted into the first sin, an ecological one, against God the Creator. Violence against creation had begun. The second garden—that of Gethsemane—is the sacred space for human redemption. The suffering and death of Christ transformed once and for all the reality of life and of all creation. Announcement of the Resurrection was celebrated in the third garden, where Christ appeared to Mary Magdalene, who mistook Him for a gardener!

For over forty years the Shaws spent their summers on Sutton Island, off the coast of Maine, a retreat whose beauty and solitude made it magnetic to members of the Harvard faculty. There Mrs. Shaw painstakingly collected notes for her "Garden Notebook," begun after she had read Rachel Carson's *Silent Spring* in 1962. That early warning of the ecological devastation also brought with it, as Mrs. Shaw states, "an understanding of the essential relatedness of all of life on planet Earth." Surrounded by the beauty of Sutton Island, Mrs. Shaw asked herself this question: "What patterns and purpose, in the Kingdom of God, relate the inner environment of the person and the endangered environment of the planet?"

Patterns and purpose, inner environment and outer environment. To these exquisite relationships, Mrs. Shaw has devoted years, and now she shares her reflections with us in *Thorns in the Garden Planet.*

A personal note here. I met Vera through the good auspices of Dr. Jung Joo Kim, a graduate of Harvard Divinity School. Indeed the witness of Dr. Kim's mother was, I am certain, instrumental in my return to Christ after twenty years of disaffection. Upon successful completion of her studies and her subsequent return to Korea, Jung Joo did not forget me. She urged Vera to give me a telephone call. Vera had no idea that I worked as Director of Communications for the North

American Coalition on Religion and Ecology (NACRE), an organization about to bring His Royal Highness Prince Phillip to America to launch a campaign for religious involvement in the environmental movement! Vera and I felt immediately that the providence of God had put the two of us together. She told me of her manuscript about religion and the environmental crisis, and after I had read it, I encouraged her to publish. I regard this introduction as a prayer of gratitude for God's blessing of strong Christian friendship in my life.

Under the leadership of Dr. Donald Conroy, NACRE believes that each of us must travel into the depths of our religious traditions and return from that journey with new motivation for working to save the earth. Because of increased religious involvement, this decade of the '90s—called the "decade of denial" by Lester Brown in his *State of the World 1992*—will witness the dawn of an ecological culture, one deeply spiritual, filled with love for our planet and longing for its healing as well as our own. There Christ will find waiting hearts. *Thorns in the Garden Planet* is the harbinger of this new dawn.

Diane E. Sherwood, Ph.D.
Washington, D.C. 1992

How Urgent Is the Problem of Environmental Pollution?

Forty thousand people recently gave evidence of how desperately the world seeks an answer to the problem of environmental pollution. From all walks of life and cultural backgrounds, they traveled to participate in the international meetings on the environment at the 1992 Earth Summit and Global Forum in Rio de Janeiro. Never in history have so many diverse people from so many countries—as well as their leaders—gathered to discuss a problem we all share: the pollution of the environment. Seven thousand members of the press attended to report these critical discussions by leaders and delegates from 176 nations. The urgent nature of the talks was underscored when several environmental groups reckoned that the following things happened during the twelve days of the Earth Summit:

- 600 to 900 plants and animals became extinct

- 482,000 acres of arable land became desert
- 1.17 million acres of tropical forest were destroyed

After developing a multitude of recommendations, the final words of the Summit were fitting: "*Let's begin!*"

As a Christian, how should I respond to environmental pollution?

Some interesting dialogue emerged at the Rio meetings that is important to Christians. The Christian Environmental Alliance sponsored a daily discussion group, "Biblical Themes on the Environment." The group raised some unsettling questions that every Christian needs to address:

- Are Christians speaking out about the Creator's care to redeem creation?
- Is the Church reminding its members that mankind was given responsibility in Eden to keep and preserve the garden?
- Where is the Church's voice on environmental issues?

Where do I begin?

As concerned Christians were challenged in these small groups, an obvious question followed: "Where do I begin?" A resounding answer echoed through the Rio stadium to the crowd gathered for a closing musical celebration: *"Begin where you live!"* A message of unity and commitment challenged the assembly:

> Tend your corner plot of the garden planet! Learn the environmental history of the area where you live, and what influences are protecting or destroying its natural beauty. Then learn to be among those who work together, as neighbors around the world, to preserve the beauty of life in the threatened garden planet![1]

I had almost finished this slim volume, *Thorns in the Garden Planet: Meditations on the Creator's Care*, before I attended the meetings in Rio de Janeiro. I heard many comments about the difficulties of getting people *who already know the existing problems* to work together to restore the environment. My thoughts returned to a quiet place on an ocean island, where, many years before, I had glimpsed the meaning of another environment—the inner environment of the human spirit. The words of George Eliot surfaced in my mind: "There is a great deal of unmapped country within us which would have to be taken into account in our explanations of our gusts and storms."[2]

This hidden environment of the human spirit is seldom mentioned in our concern for our more obvious environmental problems. We would do well to carefully reconsider this omission. Pollution of self-centeredness and self-interest in each person's inner environment needs to be recognized if we are to get to the roots of the environmental pollution of the planet. The Bible has much to say about our inner environment. Job 32:8 affirms the hidden self: "There is a spirit in man . . . [that] gives him understanding." Much of Christ's teaching concerns the pollution of this inner environment and the glad news of the renewal He offers. We need to consider how much the inner environment of the spirit and the external environment of the planet are interrelated!

Thorns in the Garden Planet is a journal of my reflections, and the reflections of others, on our Creator's care for His whole creation, including these two environments. I found the stillness of an ocean island the ideal place to meditate on God's care for us. The island provided the peaceful time I needed to linger in the gardens of the Bible and consider the Creator's redeeming pathways through the Garden of Eden, the Garden of Gethsemane, and the Garden of the Resurrection. I offer a brief description of the island so readers can sense its quietness that encourages meditation, and a glimpse of the inner environment of several islanders who protected its serenity for those who followed.

As you ponder these thoughts in unrushed stillness, my hope is that you will recognize both the thorns in our garden planet and the pollution of self-centeredness that threatens our inner environment and that you will see afresh the redeeming hope given us by our Creator God for renewal and new life in our inner and outer environments.

Chapter One

———— • ————

Reflections in Stillness

———— • ————

Be still, and know that I am God.
—Psalm 46:10

Gently, ever so softly, the mossy paths share the secrets of the island. For many years a sturdy, hand-crafted wooden notice, "Private Island," has confronted the small dock. Like an unbending sentinel, it challenges anyone who might come ashore and carelessly invade. Nearby, at the beginning of the narrow footpath that leads through the island, stands a significant, wind-weathered, sun-bleached poster.

This poster was a landmark decision of the 1970s. Designed by a talented member of the newly formed Association for the Preservation of the Island, it artistically declared the basic hopes and fears for the island's future in the midst of changing times. The poster gives public notice that the islanders are united to protect the island's beauty.

> IN FEW CORNERS OF THIS MAD WORLD IS IT POSSI-
> BLE TO MAINTAIN AN AREA UNSPOILED BY MAN'S
> THOUGHTLESSNESS.   ON OUR ISLAND WE TRY,
> AND WE ASK YOUR HELP. WE SET OUT BELOW,
> THOSE RULES AND CUSTOMS WHICH HAVE
> EVOLVED.

Ten carefully chosen, well-worded rules are set forth.

The poster's message guards the secluded pathways where quiet thoughts reach full bloom in nature's un-touched garden. Little did I realize when shiny nails first mounted this printed message what a parable the poster would become!

Years ago, those island pathways knew the fabled quiet of Indian footsteps. That was before 1755, when Ebenezer Sutton of Gloucester, Massachusetts, visited the area in search of land to settle. He talked with an Abnaki Indian who claimed to have full ownership of the lovely virgin island whose northern shoreline—fac-ing nearby Mount Desert Island—was a favored sunning place for seals. For two quarts of rum, Sutton per-suaded the Indian to give him a deed of full ownership written on a piece of birch bark. The brief account of that birch-bark deed, described in an eighteenth century letter, is preserved in the archives of the Boston Public Library.[1] The land's utter solitude proved too great a challenge for the rum-bargaining purchaser, who moved back to the security of the mainland. There is no evidence that Sutton ever lived in this wild, wonderful, wave-washed sanctuary.

A quarter-century later the challenge of island life was accepted by a few rugged settlers who were fishermen-farmers. How well they learned the harsh realities of winter isolation! So many times a well-planned dock would be demolished by one of the ocean's fierce winter fire-storms, which happen all too often along the island-dotted coastline of Maine. There is a wild rhythm to the eerie song of the whistling, winter winds. Like a powerful, possessed dervish, the ocean dances to that frenzied beat on the fragile shoreline. Man-made docks are quickly swept away in the surging swath of the storm and the icy siege of winter grips the islands.

In the rugged long-ago of island life, the early settlers defied the fury of these storms. Carefully using their best resource—their brave determination—these few, sea-seasoned settlers built a strong, sharing community that even provided a school and a small, well-chosen library to educate more than thirty children who were born on the island.

Toward the end of the nineteenth century, the solitude of the whole Mount Desert Island area was threatened by a multitude of out-of-state summer residents. They had heard wondrous reports of the unique beauty of this serene coastal area and of the town, which, on early maps, actually bore the name Eden. They traveled to the scenic coast by popular steamship lines from

Boston and New York. The great rush to buy summer land brought offers of unbelievably high prices to the original landowners. But the shrewd developers met their equals in encounters with the residents who valued their simple, outdoor life, and delighted more in their scenic heritage than in enlarged bank accounts. A number of wealthy families bought land to build large estates in the area called Eden. For some unknown reason, the name was officially changed to Bar Harbor on all later maps!

The land rush was a test of priorities. With prophets' bravery, a few far-seeing souls cried out that unchecked development would destroy the unique environment of the Mount Desert Island area. Although their opponents scoffed at the predictions, these brave people continued to warn of the long-term effects of pollution and unbridled growth, even though the coming storm cloud of pollution still seemed far away.

This last century has witnessed the fulfillment of the prophecy of an endangered environment. The once small clouds of pollution have grown and moved across the continent on the winds of man-made change. Now deadly acid rain drops on the verdant forests of Mount Desert Island. In 1989 *Time* magazine startled the world when its annual Man of the Year cover was awarded to "Endangered Earth: Planet of the Year."[2] To dramatize the urgent warning, the cover pictured planet earth tightly bound in ragged polyethylene and rope, "a fitting symbol of earth's vulnerability to man's reckless ways."

Seventy-five years earlier the July 1914 cover of *National Geographic* had offered advance warning of the earth's vulnerability. Its cover story was "The Need of Conserving the Beauty and Freedom of Nature." This featured article on environmental protection, by Charles W. Eliot, president of Harvard University, was followed by an article co-authored by three eminent scientists, "The Unique Island of Mount Desert," describing the amazing diversity of the rare flora and fauna of this island area that should be preserved.[3]

Eliot and his son, Charles Jr., recognized the uniqueness of this area in their many summers sailing together along the coast of Maine. From their first visit to Mount Desert they understood the fragile nature of the island environment with its unusual plants and peaceful beauty. In that simple island life Charles Eliot, the busy college president, found much-needed renewal of body, mind, and spirit. What an antidote to academic stress! Many years later Eliot declared, "Were it not for the summers at Mount Desert I would hardly have more time for reflective and real living than an operative in a cotton mill."[4]

Eliot believed that quiet, unrushed time for reflective thinking and meditation is essential for real living. In his eighty-fifth year he wrote from Maine to his grandchildren: "You cannot imagine how beautiful it is here. Memory doesn't keep the pictures as lovely as they really are. It is thirty years since Grandmother and I first studied these views . . . .Yet we are always surprised and freshly delighted with the loveliness of land, and sea, and woods. . . . You see that though we are old, we are still lovers. I hope you will all have the same experience. Enjoy. . . .all things beautiful. . . . . but be sure that thinking, working, and loving are the real sources of lasting happiness."[5] Eliot always stressed the need for quiet thinking. He shared my belief that reflections are best gathered in nature's quiet garden.

A master of the art of sailing, Eliot first explored the northern coast of Maine with a group of Harvard students and scientists in 1880. They pitched camp on the eastern shore of Somes Sound and made a scientific study of the abundant flora in the area. Experienced as a landscape artist, his son found the rare beauty awesome. He recommended that his busy father buy land for a summer home in this peaceful area. Later he shared with his father his dream that someday, together, they might find ways to protect the area's exquisite environment for all people to enjoy.

Tragically, in 1907 Charles Eliot, Jr. was stricken with meningitis and died. The grieving father resolved that his son's dream of preserving the wonderful beauty of Mount Desert for all people would become a reality.

The faithful development and fulfillment of those dreams was accomplished more than forty years later by a dedicated friend, George Dorr. Dorr was old and totally blind when he "saw" the hard-earned fulfillment of the young man's dreams. He established Acadia National Park, the first national park purchased with private donations and given to the United States government.[6]

The first small colony of summer residents in the isolated area of Northeast Harbor began in 1881. William Doane, Episcopal Bishop of Albany, and Charles Eliot built the first cottages. Both were men of faith who wanted a church to be built that God might be worshiped in gratitude. A small worship and Bible study group, which first met in Bishop Doane's house on Sunday mornings, grew into the Episcopal church that worships now near the shore landing. Later Eliot helped build another church. Worship of the Creator was a shared attitude in that first summer colony. In his book, *Mount Desert, A History*, George E. Street comments on the unique, reflective simplicity of the lifestyle of these first summer residents who quietly shared the beauty of the place with friends: "And one by one a bit of land was bought by people who were all of one mind, seeking real rest and the quiet, simple, outdoor natural life."[7]

These people of one mind felt the call of fulfillment and rest. Like the call of the sea, only the inner ear of the spirit could hear it. Islanders today still hear the call, gently and ever so softly, on well-worn paths, through woods, or by the sea.

Among those that heard the call of rest and simplicity were Joshua Kendall, a teacher, and George Paine, a retired Episcopal minister. Each had shed the rushed schedule of their city life to spend the summer months becoming a friend to shy birds and rare flowers. Both men willed their island homes to Harvard so that in years to come others might enjoy the island as they had. Some of their books remain in the homes, a testament to how well each man nourished the inner environment of his spirit. On a quiet walk they could easily remember poetic words like Dante's:

> The glory of Him who moves everything
> Penetrating through the universe. . . .
> The Love that moves the sun and other stars. . . .
> God's art is commonly called nature.[8]

The mile-long, woodland path between the Kendall and Paine houses passes the little cemetery, a peaceful place that shelters the last sleep of a few early islanders. George Paine chose to be buried in this simple place rather than in his famous family's prestigious plot in Mount Auburn Cemetery in Cambridge.

Thick moss silenced our footsteps the day my husband and I first took the narrow bypath to the cemetery and read the quaint words, carefully lined to fit and fill the space on each slender stone. A rusty chain enclosed the family plot of William Moore and his wife,

Eliza. Eliza's slender tombstone shares a simple yet unforgettable message:

SHE SMILED IN DEATH TO MEET HER GOD.

The happy notes of songbirds in the sheltering trees of the cemetery sounded almost like a choir! Their music added a sense of celebration to the whole cycle of life and its meaning. We lingered to read on the few smaller stones the names of little children of long ago. Beneath the names, the span of their short lives was told in years, months, and days. The stones commemorated each day of island life as precious and full of meaning.

Later, when I read Rachel Carson's *Silent Spring*, the memory of those songbirds flooded my thoughts. Carson lived much of her life and did much of her writing near the Maine coast, about seventy-five miles as the crow flies from the island. Her love of sea and land and birdsongs is so real in her writings. According to the book's jacket, she was "a trained scientist who never lost the poet's sense of wonder."[9] *Silent Spring*, containing her well-documented research on the rate at which chemical pesticides were killing birds, alerted the whole world to the increasing destruction of our environment. In dedicating the book to Albert Schweitzer, she offered a needed warning: "Man has lost the capacity to foresee and to forestall. He will end by destroying the earth."

The response to *Silent Spring* was deafening. Voices from many different lands called for help and hope in facing the growing threat to the planet. Rachel Carson's writings had helped the world understand the essential interrelatedness of all of life on planet Earth.

In 1992 a panel of twenty-two prominent Americans including Supreme Court Justice Sandra Day O'Connor, former President Jimmy Carter, columnists Russell Baker and George Will, and scientist Linus Pauling, selected *Silent Spring* as the most influential book published in the last fifty years.[10]

Rachel Carson's warning concerning the interrelatedness of life gives us reason to ponder an awesome fact: in the great vastness of the universe, only one planet—our Garden Planet—is known to have the environment capable of sustaining the loveliness of a garden. Of all the planets studied by scientists, ours is the only one found to carry its own life-supporting supply of oxygen.

Harsh predictions of the destruction of the Garden Planet seem almost unbelievable on this island of beauty and birdsongs and wonderfully fresh air. Is it really true that mankind has willfully ignored and continues to ignore the need to preserve the beauty and life of this unique planet? Why have the warnings been so widely ignored?

Why?

Is it because people don't know enough?

Or because they don't care enough?

Or is there a basic flaw in mankind that needs to be taken into account?

When I set about gathering research on the world's environmental problems, I was amazed at the ever-increasing amount of material available. Yet every year the problems have grown. And every year new warnings have been added and deeper questions asked.

Science writer Eugene Mallove raised an interesting question in his Washington Post article, "Do We Control the Universe's Fate?" He wondered, "What relation could theology have to understanding the cosmic environment?"11 He called for a search for theology dealing with the environment and the ultimate meaning of life. Quoting physicist Freeman Dyson, he added: "If our analysis of the long-range future leads us to raise questions related to the ultimate meaning and purpose of life, then let us examine these questions boldly and without embarrassment."12

I wondered about the search for a theology that relates ultimate meaning to the pollution of the environment. Is there a theology of the environment inherent in the Christian faith? As a believer, I know that an unexamined faith is not an authentic Christian faith. Is Christ's message of the kingdom of God realistic or relevant to the global discussion of the moral and ethical problems of pollution?

A very basic problem was the question of why many people failed to act in light of the knowledge they already had. Again I was reminded of George Eliot's words: "There is a great deal of unmapped country within us which would have to be taken into account in our explanations of our gusts and storms."

There is a great challenge in the inner environment of the spirit! What of its pollution? What care and concern are needed for an understanding of that important hidden environment?

The stillness of the island, like a shining reflecting pool, makes the inner environment very real. In light of that reality I can better understand the psalmist's words as he acknowledged the hidden depths of his spirit, unknown, unexplored:

> Thou art the God of the early mornings, the God of the late at nights, the God of the mountain peaks, and the God of the sea; but, my God, my soul has further horizons than the early mornings, deeper darkness than the nights of earth, higher peaks than any mountain peaks, greater depths than any sea in nature—O Thou Who art the God of all these, be my God. I cannot reach to the heights or to the depths; there are motives I cannot trace, dreams I cannot get at—my God, search me out.[13]

For a long time I reflected on the relationship of these two environments: the hidden, inner environment of the person, and the endangered environment of the planet. I remembered a number of Bible verses which emphasized that what is hidden in our heart controls our actions in all our relationships.

As I strolled the island pathways I sorted out my questions. I decided to study the biblical message about the two environments. I would also spend unrushed time meditating on the Creator's care for all His creation as seen in the three unique gardens of the Bible: The Garden of Eden, or Beginnings; the Garden of Gethsemane, or Cleansing; and the Garden of the Resurrection, or the New Creation.

Each garden tells its own story. Together they convey the eternal theme of the Creator's care for His creation. In Eden the ancient origin of sin polluted the garden's perfection and destroyed its harmony. In Gethsemane we recognize the cost of cleansing and renewing the environment. And finally, in the garden of the Resurrection, we celebrate the joyous redemption provided by the Creator Himself.

In each of the three gardens a dramatic dialogue reveals man's relationship to God, his neighbor, and himself. And in each garden the Great Questioner, who gives man so much responsibility, asks key questions. All the gifts God gives to man include accountability. The three gardens of the Bible are in a sense a dialogue between God and humanity about the care of His creation, the Garden Planet.

These meditations helped me recognize God's redeeming care for the whole world, His provision to deal with the thorns both within us and in our world, and His promise to make all things new. From Eden onward, the message of the Bible is the story of a God who seeks to fully redeem the whole creation. The Christian message offers hope for the alarming pollution of the planet as well as the inner pollution of the human spirit.

Questions:

How does my belief in God, as Creator, affect the way I think about serious environmental problems in the Garden Planet?

What practical examples can I give of the way my faith in the Creator affects:

(a) My priorities in the way I care for creation?

(b) My daily habits in the way I use the creation?

(c) My happiness in the way I enjoy creation?

Chapter Two

———— · ————

The Ecology of Eden

———— · ————

*Then God saw everything that He had
made, and indeed it was very good.*
—Genesis 1:31

*Then the Lord God took the man and put
him in the garden of Eden to tend and
keep it.*
—Genesis 2:15

In the first sentence of his famous essay on gardens,
the seventeenth-century scholar Francis Bacon wrote:
"God planted the first Garden, and this is the purest
pleasure."[1] Bacon's essay reflects attitudes about gardens that were prevalent in the days of luxurious estates,
where landscaping by hired laborers made exquisite
designs that extended for acres. Bacon saw such gardens as the ideal, and noted that they should have a

large central mount that was high enough to allow an overview of the far-reaching patterns.

If we use Bacon's ideal garden as an analogy, Eden, too, has a garden mount with an extended view of man in relation to his environment in the Garden Planet. The view reveals eternal meanings and patterns in man's relationship to himself, his neighbor, and his God. Bacon found powerful symbolism in the vista of a garden mount, and its picturesque view delighted him. He enjoyed his own garden as a parable of God's creation.

In his book, *God in Creation: A New Theology of Creation and the Spirit of God*, Jürgen Moltmann points out that theology always encourages an invigorating exercise of the imagination. "If we were to ban the images of the imagination from theology," he says, "we would be robbing it of its best possession."[2]

The power of the imagination enriches the images of so many stories. Christ, the Great Storyteller, generously used stories and parables to help ordinary people sense something of God's extraordinary glory and His amazing grace. Vivid imagery fills both the Old and New Testaments. But with characteristic realism, the Bible reminds its readers that the imagination can be used for evil as well as good. An early chapter in the book of Genesis describes God's concern for the increase of wickedness in the heart of man and says that every intent of the imaginations of his heart "was only evil continually"(Gen. 6:5). In recognition of the power of the mind, the greatest Law asks that we love

God with our minds (Luke 10:27). An imagination that loves God can make the imagery of the biblical message a constant joy!

The Creation story abounds in luminous imagery. The ageless words of Hebrew poetry make the story of the Garden of Beginnings relevant to people of every age and culture. Those who spend hours fussing to formulate a date to impose on the first chapter of Genesis miss the celebrative imagery of the Creation narrative.

The opening chapter of Genesis focuses on the Creator's joyful blessing given to each successive stage of His creation. How often do we remind ourselves of the deep satisfaction and joy God experienced in His acts of creation? (Sometime, when you're enjoying a beautiful sunset, consider the Creator's joy as the beauty of His design was fulfilled.) After each stage of Creation, "God saw that it was good!" (Gen. 1:10,12,18,20,25). And what enthusiasm is expressed in that final verse: "God saw everything that He had made, and indeed it was very good" (Gen.1:31).

The Sabbath was the crowning celebration of Creation. It was the day the Creator rested and examined and enjoyed the completion of the universe. The imagery in the Genesis description is of a great artist who has just completed a masterpiece and stands back to observe his handiwork, enjoying each detail of its loveliness. Only the Master Artist can fully understand and interpret His handiwork. On the first Sabbath He celebrated His accomplishment and placed a special blessing on the day of rest. God commanded His people to take a weekly, rest-filled day to remember the Creation, "For in six days the Lord made the heavens and the earth, the sea, and all that is in them, and rested the seventh day. Therefore the Lord blessed the Sabbath day and hallowed it" (Ex. 20:11). He wanted to insure that this quiet rest, which celebrates creation in the Creator's way, might never be forgotten.

The Genesis story emphasizes the humble beginnings of the human body created from dust and the holy beginnings of the human spirit, formed by the breath of God. After creating, in vast diversity, the creatures of sea, sky, and land, the Creator revealed a unique purpose: "Let Us make man in Our image, according to our likeness" (Gen. 1:26). From "the dust of the ground" the Master Designer created the human body, and breathed into it His breath of life, and "man became a living being" (Gen. 2:7). Calling man "an animal" ignores the image he bears and the spirit given to him by God. Meditate on the life-changing truth that we are all created in the image of our Maker so that we might walk with Him and eternally enjoy intimate fellowship with our Father and Creator.

Many of David's psalms convey something of the Creator's joy on that first Sabbath. The beauty of his serene environment awed the young, solitary shepherd who guarded his sleeping sheep as he studied the pathways of the stars. His song in the night—Psalm 8—celebrated his joyous appreciation of the Master

Artist. The author of Proverbs echoes the Maker's joy in His masterpiece when he writes of the wisdom of Creation:

> The Lord possessed me at the beginning of His way,
> Before His works of old.
> I have been established from everlasting,
> From the beginning, before there was ever an earth.
> When there were no depths I was brought forth,
> When there were no fountains abounding with water.
> Before the mountains were settled,
> Before the hills, I was brought forth;
> While as yet He had not made the earth or the fields,
> Or the primal dust of the world.
> When He prepared the heavens, I was there,
> When He drew a circle on the face of the deep,
> When He established the clouds above,
> When He strengthened the fountains of the deep,
> When He assigned to the sea its limit,
> So that the waters would not transgress His command,
> When He marked out the foundations of the earth,
> Then I was beside Him, as a master craftsman;
> And I was daily His delight,
> Rejoicing always before Him,
> Rejoicing in His inhabited world,
> And my delight was with the sons of men.
>
> Prov. 8:22-31

The Genesis story does not emphasize the beginning of man's body, or the date of that beginning! Rather the emphasis is that man, made in the image of God, is uniquely alive. He is a living soul who was created to live with God in the Garden. Augustine understood the great purpose and love expressed in the creation of man when he said: "Thou has made us for Thyself; our hearts are restless till we find our rest in Thee."[3]

The story of Eden is the story of mankind's relationship with an ideal environment and with the Creator of that environment. In the perfectly balanced ecology of Eden, during the days when man walked there with God, the Creator shared His dominion over the Garden with man. God gave man the wonderful responsibility to till and keep the garden. (The Hebrew word for "keep" can also be translated "preserve.") Man's responsibility to preserve the environment was an important part of the harmony of Eden. It is a beautiful image—the sovereign Lord created His masterpiece and then created one made in His image to preserve and care for the garden. How much He loved mankind to want to share His handiwork! What a joy for Adam to be given the high honor of keeping God's own creation.

But Man lost his right of dominion, and the reason for that loss is an important part of the Eden story. God gave Man (Adam and Eve) the whole Garden to enjoy as home. At the center of the Garden stood the Tree of Life, glorious in the full meaning of its fruit. Beside it stood the Tree of the Knowledge of Good and Evil. The Creator generously encouraged man to freely enjoy the fruit of the garden with only one important restriction. He warned that the fruit of the Tree of the Knowledge of Good and Evil was toxic. Eating that fruit would destroy something essential in man; it would pollute his inner environment. "For in the day that you eat of it you shall surely die" (Gen.2:17). The Hebrew verb for "die" used in this passage denotes a continuing, progressive action—something in man would begin to die as soon as he rebelled against the guidelines of the Garden and ate the fruit. But the dying would accelerate until the full effect of rebellion against the Creator's guidelines of the Garden resulted in ultimate pollution: death.

The story of Eden gives amazing insight into environmental problems. While surrounded by the abundance of the perfect environment, enjoying all its wonderful resources, man decided that no restrictions should limit his control. His fascination with evil polished the forbidden fruit. Man believed all creation was for his satisfaction, and he alone should decide how to use it.

And so, in this Garden of Beginnings, man chose to disregard the warnings of what would follow the misuse of creation and purposely ignored God's command not to eat the fruit. He decided to make his choices based on his own presuppositions. The forbidden fruit was "a delight to the eyes" that would enable him to "be like God, knowing good and evil" (Gen. 3:5). He thought he had the chance to become his own god, and determined he could decide for himself what was right and what was wrong!

Perhaps abundance blinds us to our basic need for God, for misuse of the environment began in the midst of Eden's abundance and harmony. Adam walked away from God and chose the fatal fruit of self-gratification. He suddenly felt ashamed and insecure. He knew harmony with God had been lost, and everything in the Garden seemed changed. He knew he had changed, too—on the inside. And so he hid from God.

The central theme of *Thorns in the Garden Planet* is the Creator's desire to redeem and renew His creation. In the midst of the shattered harmony of Eden, God sought a renewed relationship. Today with the same quiet question he asked Adam, "Where are you?" (Gen. 3:9) He asks mankind to respond, and to admit just where we are. This very first question recorded in Scripture, directed to man by the seeking God, reads ironically in a contemporary culture that seems to ask disinterestedly, "Where in the world is God?"

The Great Questioner reminded Adam of the divine law that protected the whole ecology of Eden. The Creator was the one who asked the first question concerning man's attitude toward his environment. And man, to whom God gave the power of choice and the power of reason, had to respond. He was forced to take responsibility for his choice to disregard God's guidelines for the Garden. His attitude threatened the whole beauty of creation. By his own rebellious choice, man forfeited his privilege of dominion and was banished from Eden. Instead of living in the glorious harmony of the Garden, man had to till the ground bearing the terrible curse of his rebellion against the Creator. Thorns, the symbol of that curse, would spring up to taunt and remind him that he no longer had dominion.

As Adam and Eve left the Garden of Beginnings together, sharp thorns filled the dark, unknown paths ahead. Thorns, the obvious result of their rebellion, would be part of their world for as long as they lived. An angel stood at the Garden's entrance, guarding it with a flashing sword. There was no way back to the harmony of all creation and the path to the Tree of Life.

One enigma of the Eden story is why Adam and Eve didn't choose to eat from the healthy Tree of Life, in all its fruitfulness, rather than the poisonous fruit of the Tree of the Knowledge of Good and Evil. They came to realize the deep meaning of the power of choice. As they left the beautiful environment of Eden, they recognized the problems they must face and that all their descendants have faced throughout time—thorns in the garden planet.

Questions:

How does the Garden of Beginnings help us recognize:
(a) the Creator's care for all creation?
(b) the Creator's loving attitude to all people in His creation?

What responsibilities and privileges were given to each individual in Eden?

What does it mean to be made "in the image of God"?

How does Eden help each of us recognize the "inner environment" of our spirit?

Chapter Three

———— · ————

The Goal of Garden Relationships

———— · ————

I bow my knees to the Father . . . from whom the whole family in heaven and earth is named, that He would grant you, according to the riches of His glory, to be strengthened with might through His Spirit in the inner man. . .
—Ephesians 3:14-16

Early Eden portrays man in perfect harmony in his most basic relationships: with God, with another person, and with himself. It is essential for man to understand what God intended for these relationships in order to live harmoniously with all creation.

Quietly meditating on the actual meaning of "made in the image of God" is an awesome experience! We find the identities God intended for us in the Garden of Beginnings: each person is a unique individual bearing the image of God! Since we all have such an identity, is it any wonder God asks us to love (not worship) ourselves, gratefully treasuring ourselves as He created us to be? In this spirit He calls us to love our neighbors as ourselves, for they, too, are made in the image of God. Eden illustrates that this harmony is centered in God: "in Him we live and move and have our being" (Acts 17:28).

What pattern and purpose for life we find in the Garden of Beginnings! Eden's beauty and harmony have been celebrated for centuries in music, art, and literature. Look at Michelangelo's portrayal of God's hand stretching out to reach the newly created Adam, waking him to life. Listen with heart as well as ear to the music of Haydn's majestic *Creation*. And meditate on the powerful stanzas of Milton's *Paradise Lost*. How impoverished our civilization would be—and our whole concept of life—without these great artistic reminders of the Creator's work in the Garden of Beginnings.

In 1964 James Fisher and Roger Tory Peterson published their famous book, *The World of Birds*, with updated statistics on environmental pollution. Quoting *Paradise Lost* they indicated man himself was the problem! They emphasized the need for a spiritual dimension in the search for answers.

The 1988 government report of Fisheries and Wildlife Conservation and the Environment issued a sterner alert. Rachel Carson was working with this same government agency when she collected the material for *Silent Spring*. Thirty-six years after Carson's warning, this agency's report stated: "The earth is nearing a stage of extinction of species unequaled since the age of the dinosaurs. Scientists estimate that one plant or animal species is currently being lost per day worldwide and that by the end of the decade the extinction rate may rise to one species per hour."[1] (Note the 1992 rate of increasing destruction reported at the Earth Summit, as mentioned in the Prologue.)

Fisher and Peterson had predicted the inevitable results of man's unabated environmental pollution:

> Man has become the most dangerous, the most lethal animal upon the face of the earth. Poisonous, he can through his endless proliferation of toxic chemicals, change his venom, a thing no snake can do. But he may not be immune to his own venom. . . polluting the streams, the sea and the air. We believe that now man has the power to destroy nature and himself almost totally. He has been compelled to make a searing assessment of himself; of his own aggressiveness, greed, power and impact. The extinction [of species] is the responsibility of man, not nature . . .a reproach to human civilization; an indicator of the grave extent in which man's role in nature's network is uneasy and maladjusted.

> Accuse not Nature, she hath done her part:
> Do thou but thine, and be not diffident
> Of wisdom, she deserts thee not, if thou dismiss not her.

> Let us, on our way to paradise regained, pause to learn
> lessons from the fate of birds . . . It is not so much a question
> of nature's rights as of man's duty.[2]

Thus three hundred years after Milton wrote those poetic lines about man's duty toward nature (and nearly seven hundred years after Dante wrote his poem about the great loss of Eden) concerned scientists quoted *Paradise Lost*, using the illustration of Eden to help man recognize his responsibility in the Garden Planet.

The poetry of Milton and Dante was well represented in fireside books at the turn of the century. During those days people on the island enjoyed reading aloud around an evening fire. A three-volume set of *The Divine Comedy*, loaned by our neighbor George Paine, was already well-worn, with many passages underlined, long before we ever arrived on the island. What fascinating stories this ninety-year-old islander could tell of the heated discussions in his college days (class of 1896) about the philosophy of *Paradise Lost* and *The Divine Comedy*. Around the turn of the century, many college students wrote papers questioning man's right relationship with Nature, as expressed in these great books. Many wondered: What is the importance of man's will in response to God's will? Often the students quoted Dante's words:

> The greatest gift that God in His bounty made in creation,
> and the most comfortable to His goodness, and that which
> He prizes the most, was the freedom of the will, with which
> the creatures with intelligence are endowed.[3]

Many students included other lines from Dante:

And in His will is our tranquility:
It is the mighty ocean, whither tends,
Whatever it creates and nature makes.[4]

The Creative Will that designed the environment of
Eden and created man in His image is praised in many
other poems and in many other languages. The art,
music, and literature of Western civilization celebrates
the divine drama of creation: the story of man's first
relationships with his Creator, his companion, his conscience, and the virgin environment of creation. Often
unmentioned, in retelling the Eden story, is that man
expressed his first rebellion against God in his relationship to creation, rather than in his relationship with
other people. Man's self-centered attitude in wanting
to use creation in whatever way suited his desires was
the first fatal flaw that eventually endangered the whole
environment of the Garden Planet.

The vivid details of mankind's creation make this a
fascinating story of relationships. Following the description of the creation of the universe in the opening
chapter of Genesis, the second chapter offers further
details of the unique creation of both Adam and Eve.
Adam was formed first from the dust of the earth and
God breathed into him, and man became a living soul
bearing God's image.

This very uniqueness, set apart by his living spirit
inbreathed by God, separated Adam from the rest of

creation. In all the Garden no other creatures could comprehend or communicate the living image of God. There was no companion with whom Adam could share the glorious meaning of life. In his uniqueness, Adam was lonely. And the God who said, "Let Us make man in Our image"(Gen. 1:26) had compassion on Adam in his aloneness. He said, "It is not good that man should be alone; I will make him a helper comparable to him" (Gen. 2:18). The rich meaning of the Hebrew word translated *helper* is easily overlooked. This same word is used in Psalms to describe the nurturing, helpful nature of God:

> I will lift up my eyes to the hills—
> From whence comes my help?
> My help comes from the Lord,
> Who made heaven and earth.
>
> Ps. 121:1-2

The word *helper* in the Eden story has no connotation of "servant" but rather a person whose active companionship fittingly enriches every dimension of living.   Thus Eden is the place of companionship blessed by God. The meaning of relationships is central in the Garden of Beginnings.

Jonathan Edwards emphasized that the ultimate meaning of relationships is found in God's own nature.[5] In fact Edwards described the wondrous holiness of God in terms of the beauty of those very relationships—called "the Trinity"—within Himself. It was in the glory of those relationships that God created man in His image.

Some copies of Edwards' writings, and an early edition of the private journal of his daughter Esther, were among the old books already in our island house when my husband and I arrived. Esther Edwards' journal,[6] written in her youth, reveals her father's great enjoyment of nature as the handiwork of God and of his dedication to excellence in scholarship as he studied the great truths of the Christian faith. Edwards' life exemplified the spirit celebrated by the plaque at the main gate to Harvard yard, which affirms the spiritual meaning of Harvard's beginnings:

> After God had carried us safe to New England, and we had builded our houses, provided necessaries for our livelihood, reared convenient places for God's worship, and settled the civil government: one of the next things we longed for, and looked after was to advance Learning and perpetuate it to posterity, dreading to leave an illiterate ministry to the churches, when our present ministers shall lie in the dust.[7]

When Yale Press reprinted the writings of Jonathan Edwards in 1966, he was described as America's greatest philosopher. And how greatly his appreciation of creation influenced his life and thinking! Even in the quiet of the island, we found Edwards' profound writings on philosophy and theology slow, difficult reading. But the island was a wonderful place to read his description, in eighteenth-century language, of creation as the expression of God's glory:

> I walked abroad, alone, in a solitary place . . . . looking upon the sky and clouds, there came into my mind a sweet sense of the glorious majesty and grace of God as I know not how to express . . . Majesty and meekness joined together; it was a sweet and gentle, and holy majesty; a majestic meekness . . .a great and holy gentleness.
>
>   After this my sense of divine things gradually increased . . . and had more of that inward sweetness. The appearance of every thing was altered; there seemed to be . . . [the] calm, sweet appearance of divine glory in almost everything. God's excellence, his wisdom, his purity and love seemed to appear in everything; in the sun, moon, and stars; in the clouds and blue sky, in the grass, flowers, and trees; in the water and all nature . . . I spent much time viewing . . . to behold the sweet glory of God in these things, singing forth in a low voice, my contemplations of the Creator and Redeemer.[8]

These meditations on the Creator's glory encouraged us to read more of Edwards' writings. A brilliant young Harvard graduate student, Krister Sairsingh, gave us glimpses into the meanings of Edwards' theology. Sairsingh was preparing his Ph.D. thesis entitled "Jonathan Edwards and the Idea of Divine Glory: His Foundational Trinitarianism and Its Ecclesial Import."[9] Sairsingh explained his reflections on the oft-quoted words, "Let Us make man in Our image" in a follow-up article published in a special edition of *Veritas Reconsidered*:

From Edwards, I have learned that God's holiness has to do with the beauty of relationships—the relationships within God's triune life. God's holiness is expressed in the mutual love of Father, Son, and Holy Spirit . . . If God is holy it is because of the beauty of communion and the perfection of this love relationship within the Trinity. God's holiness then is not something distinct from God's sociality. And if we humans are to attain any measure of holiness, Edwards urges, it will be through our relationship to the triune God and the expression of God's love in all our human relationships. Holiness is a social reality.[10]

That the glory of God is expressed in relationships gives a wonderful dimension to the story of the creation of Eve. Adam would find in her a companion who was also made in the image of God. Eve's name and nature reflected God's understanding of her need for a respected identity. To achieve shared identity the Creator started with nothing less than an integral part of Adam, a rib, to create woman, whose body would be comparable to and compatible with Adam's. Appreciating what that really meant, after his lonely search throughout all creation for an understanding companion, Adam welcomed Eve:

> "This is now bone of my bones
> And flesh of my flesh,
> She shall be called Woman,
> Because she was taken out of Man."
>   Gen. 2:23

This sense of oneness that Adam understood and appreciated, allows no room for the theory that the Eden story describes women as inferior. Adam and Eve were created with mutual respect for all they shared together in the basic relationships of family life. They were reminded that children, too, were unique individuals developing lives of their own in the security of unselfish family love, and would later leave their parents to make their own commitments in marriage.

It is interesting to note that the relationship of marriage is offered as an illustration of the Church as the bride of Christ who is loyally and lovingly devoted to Him. Using this illustration, in writing to the church at Ephesus, the apostle Paul said: "Husbands, love your wives, just as Christ also loved the church and gave Himself for it" (Eph. 5:25).

In fact the beauty of every relationship within the human family is used in Scripture to illustrate Christ's redeeming love at work in the lives of believers: husband and wife, parent and child, and brother and sister. We recognize the basic strength of the family in the continuing commitment of marriage. The Eden story speaks of the shared oneness in marriage: "Therefore a man shall leave his father and mother and be joined to his wife, and they shall become one flesh" (Gen. 2:24).

Centuries later, Christ quoted these very words. He was talking to a crowd when someone decided the question of divorce would be a dandy way to make a fool of His teaching about marriage: "Why then did

Moses command to give a certificate of divorce, and put [his wife] away?" (Matt. 19:7).

I bet the man who asked that question in front of all the listening crowd thought he'd show how little Jesus understood the latest attitude toward divorce. Jesus replied: "Moses, because of the hardness of your hearts, permitted you to divorce your wives, but from the beginning it was not so" (Matt. 19:8). The flaw, explained Jesus, was not in the master-design of marriage in Eden. That design was planned and protected in the pattern of the greatest law of love. A Christian marriage recognized that nothing less than the love of God, Himself, had joined them together. The flaw was in the hardness of their hearts. Jesus often reminded the crowds that the hard problems of society began in the hidden hardness of the heart—that precious, fragile, inner environment. Like a lovely garden path, the soil of a heart could be so trampled to hardness there remained no room for growth.

It was Eve who first spoiled the master plan of creation. She decided she would use the creation to satisfy her own desires as she saw fit. After all, she saw the fruit of the forbidden tree "was good for food" and "desirable to make one wise" (Gen. 3:6).

She decided to make her own choice. Her self-interest must have top priority in this beautiful environment the Creator had said He wanted to protect. After she ate, she gave some to her husband. Together they used Eden to suit their own desires and purposes. Too late they realized the harmony of the Garden had been destroyed.

At the heart of the Eden story is the tragedy of broken human relationships. Forever after, man would have to deal with the thorns resulting from broken relationships with his Creator, his companion, his inner environment, and eventually the environment of the whole Garden Planet.

Questions:

What are your favorite examples in art, music and literature as expressions of God's glory in creation?

Which Psalms help you enjoy the greatness of God's work in creation?

What relationship and attitude does the Creator seek for each of us:
- (a) to have with Him?
- (b) to have with ourself?
- (c) to have with those around us?

Chapter Four

———— • ————

The Tragedy of Broken Relationships

———— • ————

To a great many people the traditional language of Christians has become meaning-less . . . .They scarcely know what we mean by the word sin . . . .The essence of man's sin is his self-centeredness.
—William Temple

For what will it profit a man if he gains the whole world, and loses his own soul?
—Mark 8:36

By his own choice and actions, man lost the special relationships given to him by the Creator. The curse of broken relationships about which he had been fully warned began polluting the whole environment. He could no longer live in the harmony of the environment of Eden. Gone was the unbroken fellowship of walking in the garden with God. Gone was the harmony in his own soul! Gone, too, was the privilege of dominion that God had shared with him in Eden. The loss of dominion and the reason for that loss, is an important part of the story of the Garden of Beginnings. It provides insight for today's problems of pollution in the Garden Planet.

Theologians give the name "original sin" to Adam's refusal to accept God's guidelines for life with Him in the Garden. But today sin is seldom mentioned as an underlying cause of our problems. William Temple, Archbishop of Canterbury, commented on this modern refusal to think in terms of sin:

> To a great many people the traditional language of Christians has become unmeaning. It does not fit in with their way of looking at life. They scarcely know what we mean by the word sin, supposing sin to consist of consciously doing what is known or believed to be wrong. But this is only one part of the whole great fact of sin—the invisible part, so to speak. It is the symptom, not the disease . . . . The essence of man's sin is his self-centeredness.[1]

Because sin itself is invisible—only its effects can be seen—people often deny its reality. Radioactive poisoning is an illustration of the progressive, although invisible, effects of a highly toxic influence. The presence of radiation is not detectable by any of man's five senses. A person cannot recognize this danger with his natural senses; he can neither see, hear, smell, taste, or touch the reality of radioactivity. It can be detected only by special instruments and film. Before a scientist enters a room in which radioactive compounds may be present, he must wear a test-badge containing film sensitive to radioactivity. Only after the film is developed is the presence of life-threatening radiation known. These precautions are necessary to overcome the limitations of man's natural senses, even though modern man has placed great confidence in his natural abilities. The warning test-badge itself must be carefully maintained, with frequent changes of film to ensure its reliability.

The deadly invisibility of radioactivity caused the horrible terror of Chernobyl, both immediately and continuing still. The worldwide dimension of the toxicity of Chernobyl became the silent, invisible horror that threatened peace of mind for millions of thinking people around the world. How far would this pollution extend? Even thousands of miles from the original site where radioactivity was released into the atmosphere investigators found cow's milk containing the deadly poison. But just as man's natural senses couldn't detect the release of the poison, neither could man's senses detect its spread. That could be demonstrated only by special instruments. If man depended only on the reasoning of natural senses, he would never comprehend the reality or its threat to his life.

Radioactivity is an awesome illustration of some of the characteristics of sin. How do you define or recognize sin? It is not detectable in terms of man's natural senses. Like radioactivity, sin's visible effects may convince some people of its dangers, while others may scoff at any evidence of its reality. Dr. Karl Menninger, well recognized for his leadership in professional counseling, wrote *Whatever Became of Sin?*[2] In this book Menninger emphasizes the need to recognize the reality of sin and sinfulness in modern society and in our individual lives. Like the radioactive sensitive film scientists must wear to confirm contamination, each human being has a built-in test badge that indicates the pollution of his inner environment caused by sin. That built-in test badge is his conscience. After Adam read his test badge of accountability, he said: "I was afraid . . . and I hid" (Gen. 3:10). What theologians call original sin was Adam saying to the Creator: I will use your creation for whatever purpose serves my self-interest and my own goals. The pollution of man's spirit—his inner environment—by self-centeredness would eventually affect the whole world and its environment. Like Chernobyl, sin's effects might be recognized only by those who, in their study of the environment, included a reference to test badges. The long life of radioactive poisoning is well recognized as a danger for generations to come. How true this is of sin! The Ten Commandments warn us that sin's toxic effects continue even "to the third and fourth generations" (Ex. 20:5).

The Creator warned Adam and Eve of the continuing, long-term effects of the self-centeredness of their lives.

If they were allowed to remain in Eden, it would change the whole ecology and destroy the harmony. Their decision to center their lives in themselves rather than in God changed the relationship of all things. Because they were unique individuals, the Creator expressed the different ways their selfishness would affect their lives, their families and eventually the extended family on the Garden Planet.

Adam would labor to till and keep land that no longer had the blessing of harmony: Even the ground is changed . . ."cursed is the ground because of you . . . . Thorns will spring up . . . With the sweat of your brow you shall live . . . In toil you will eat . . . until you return to the dust from which you came" (Gen. 3:17-19 NIV).

Eve learned that her sorrow would be different. As a woman her strengths lay in the likeness of her nature to the nurturing nature of God. Therefore, what would be most painful to her would not be thorns growing in the Planet, but tears in the family. She would grieve for the cumulative effects of self-centeredness and self-interest in her family and extended family. The first part of the warning, "I will greatly increase your pains in childbearing," was the short-term problem of labor pain. But the next phrase, "with pain you will give birth to children," was a continuing, long-term problem that could refer to adult children, even those of future generations, whose self-centeredness would spoil loving relationships within the family and the world community (Gen.3:16, NIV).

How meaningful is the name given to Eve, "the mother of all living" (Gen. 3:20). Anthropologists who study the genetic history of the human race recognize the continuity of the human family which can be traced from its founding mother. The Garden of Beginnings predates modern terms such as *genes, chromosomes,* and *mitochondrial (mt) DNA* which these scientists use in tracing the family tree of humanity. A fascinating article, "The Unmasking of Mitochondrial Eve," states: "Because mitochondria pass from generation to generation only through the female line . . . the mtDNA data essentially trace female inheritance. Ultimately, a single female is reached at the root of the tree; hence the reference to Eve."[3] The exact identity of mitochondrial Eve evokes much discussion. Reserch verifies that in humans mitochondria pass from one generation to the next only through mothers. This unique role of women in the genetic history of the whole race affirms the honoring of Eve as "the mother of all living."

The master design borne by every person in each succeeding generation includes more than Eve's imprint on our hidden genes. The master design also includes the imprint of God's image on the environment of the human spirit. Even from the Garden of Beginnings God emphasized the internal spiritual environment in the relationships of family life. Children were regarded as "a gift of the Lord" (Ps. 127:3 NAS; Isa. 8:18). Jesus spoke highly of the worth of each child in the kingdom of God and of each child's need for individual, spiritual nourishment (Matt. 19:14; John 21:15). Early in the Eden story, before children were born to Adam and Eve, the Creator pointed out that parents do not "own" their children. They have years of opportunity to help nourish the inner environment of each child with family love, but the goal is to help each child mature and find his or her own fulfillment in God's image.

But before Adam and Eve left the Garden of Beginnings they were given the prophecy of good news. The Eternal Ecologist would provide the needed answers to the thorns in the planet garden and the tears in the planet family. Someday the Messiah—the cleansing Christ—would be born of a woman (Gen. 3:15). He would finally deal with the problem of pollution. He would bring the message and the means to deliver the planet garden and the planet family from the ever-growing problems of pollution.

The last family portrait in the Garden of Beginnings is a masterpiece. It portrays the Caring Parent kneeling down to the children's eye level, helping the children learn to dress for school. A warm coat is needed, for the winds outside can blow cold and cruel. Ahead of them are some long hard lessons about pollution in the Garden Planet. The Caring Parent helps them dress for school: "for Adam and his wife the Lord God made tunics of skin, and clothed them" (Gen. 3:21).

They had so much to learn!

The day they were banished from Eden was filled with sorrow. And all too soon after they left the garden, Adam and Eve saw the polluting effects of sin within the environment of their own family. During a fit of anger their oldest son killed his brother in an open field. God, who is continually portrayed in the Bible as the Great Questioner, asked Cain, "Where is Abel your brother?" Cain denied knowing about his brother and asked in defiance, "Am I my brother's keeper?" With an eerie reminder that the whole environment of life is defiled by hate and murder, the Great Questioner asked, "What have you done? The voice of your brother's blood cries out to Me from the ground. So now you are cursed from the earth" (Gen. 4:9-11). In a strange sense the ground beyond Eden now bears the tragic harvest of hate and alienation within the planet family. Eve must have remembered the earlier warning that sorrow would be hers when she saw the effects of self-centered sin in the lives of her children. She had been told that family life would be different. How very much self-centeredness had changed her relationship to God, to her husband, and now to their children! The harmony of their family relationships had been destroyed.

Beyond Eden the thorns of self-interest would become an ever-increasing ecological problem, finally extending even to outer space. Man's refusal to center his life in God continues to destroy his communion with creation.

Questions:

How meaningful do you find William Temple's definition of sin as "self-centeredness"?

How do you define sin?

Why is recognition of the inner environment in each person important in order to deal with the environmental problems of the planet?

How does self-centeredness affect your relationship to

  (a) God?
  (b) yourself?
  (c) those near you?
  (d) creation?

———— • ————

Chapter Five

The Sabbath Rest: Renewal for Man and Nature

———— • ————

In returning and rest shall you be saved;
In quietness and confidence shall be your
strength.

—Isaiah 30:15

Ever since the gate of Eden was closed, the way back to the Tree of Life has been barred. Lest man seek to enter by force, an angel with a flaming sword has guarded the gate. And ever since, deep in his heart, man has yearned for the harmony he knew there. He has longed for a Messiah who would come with healing for all relationships in creation, and especially in the family; a Messiah who could deal with the sword at the closed gate to the Tree of Life. In that light, the words of the prophet Malachi become more meaningful:

> "The Sun of Righteousness shall arise
> With healing in His wings . . .And He will turn
> The hearts of the fathers to the children,
> And the hearts of the children to their fathers."
>
> Mal.4:2, 6

The messianic traditions of both Jews and Christians look forward to resolving the disharmony between God, humanity, and nature. Creation and relationships are closely linked throughout Scripture. The apostle Paul described the powerful relationship between man and nature in his letter to the Romans, emphasizing that renewal of the earth is inextricably linked to man's renewal:

> For the creation was subjected to futility, not willingly, but because of Him who subjected it in hope; because the creation itself also will be delivered from the bondage of corruption into the glorious liberty of the children of God.
>
> Rom. 8:20,21

In 1962, just as *Silent Spring* was published and the environmental movement was in its infancy, George Williams wrote about the scriptural background for the Christian role in conservation and stewardship of natural resources.[1] In lectures at Gordon-Conwell Theological Seminary, he called for Christians—with their sense of the Creator and creation—to become messengers of the Christian attitude to nature. He asked "Who can better mount the watchtower and sound the alert for the care of the earth?"[2]

The heritage of Scripture includes a love for the whole creation. God's delight in his creation in Genesis is carried forward in the garden themes throughout the Old and New Testaments and culminates in the book of Revelation when access to the Tree of Life is restored: "In the middle . . .was the tree of life, which bore twelve fruits . . .for the healing of the nations" (Rev.22:2). Sadly, the church today has generally neglected her responsibility to cherish and defend nature.

What attitude is commonly held today regarding man's relationship to creation? Many Christians claim dominion of the natural resources of the Garden Planet, but that assertion misses the meaning of man's banishment from the Garden of Beginnings. Even though man was banished from the perfectly balanced environment of the Garden—and that proved to be a significant loss—it was not his greatest loss. Even worse, he lost the dominion the Creator so generously shared with him. Forever after, thorns have challenged man as he seeks to till and keep the Garden Planet and toils to earn the bread he needs for sustenance.

Years ago Rachel Carson rightly objected to man's arrogance in claiming dominion over the natural environment.[3] And Moltmann has referred to the tendency in the Western world for some people of the Christian tradition to believe the early chapters of Genesis support man's claim to do whatever he wants with the earth's resources because he has the right of dominion over all the earth.[4]   Moltmann points out how very detrimental this error in thinking has been to ecological harmony.   Unfortunately we are seldom reminded that man's right to dominion, described in the Genesis story, was abrogated because of self-interest.   Dominion became toil.   Inherent in the toil necessary for daily survival was the challenge of tilling ground bearing thorns.

Man's struggle with the environment had begun!

But in the midst of the struggle, the Creator called for a weekly celebration: a day of rest for man and beast and all creation!   God decreed the Sabbath as a day of unrushed rest for man to remember that day the Creator had rested on the Sabbath and enjoyed all his works.   The Sabbath was a special gift man was to take from Eden.

"God blessed the seventh day and sanctified it" (Gen. 2:3).   In doing so, He made rest a part of creation.   This full and final blessing was pronounced on the day of rest when the Creator celebrated the goodness and greatness of creation.   Mankind was to remember the Sabbath Day and keep it holy.   The word used in Scripture to describe keeping the Sabbath is the same one used for man's responsibility to keep the Garden and means to "preserve" what has already been made lovely.

Moltmann makes an important point about the way Western churches present the creation and the relation of the Sabbath to it. Many churches confine creation to the six days of God at work, and neglect to present "the resting God, the celebrating God, the God who rejoiced over His creation,"[5] who used the Sabbath as "the feast of creation."[6] In giving the Ten Commandments at Sinai, God made His intention for the Sabbath more clear. The commandment concerning the Sabbath is the longest and most detailed. Thus, in the midst of what man is commanded to do, he is asked to remember the goodness of what God did in creation and to acknowledge and use the gift of rest.

In remembering we refresh the inner environment of our spirits so we can deal with problems in the Garden Planet. Moltmann emphasizes that the Sabbath rest "completes and crowns" the creation saying, "It is the Sabbath which blesses, sanctifies, and reveals the world as God's creation."[7] And Moltmann reminds us of Gese's comment on the Sabbath that puts God's commands in perspective. "The main purpose [of the day of rest] is the non-intervention of human beings in the environment . . . In principle, what is at stake is the inviolability of creation, which at least on every seventh day is to be preserved from man, as a sign and symbol."[8]

In 1973 my husband and I experienced five Israeli Sabbaths. We were in Israel to participate in a five-week seminar on "The Jewish Sources of Christianity: Literary and Archeological" sponsored by Hebrew Union College. After six days of a very busy schedule filled with long hours in archeological digs and class-room lectures, the unrushed quiet of the Sabbath was refreshing. In that setting, we understood the original meaning of the Sabbath and the blessing pronounced on it. We came to understand more clearly that the compassionate Creator gave the Sabbath to everyone, whether rich or poor, that each might have the unde-niable right to a day of rest. If the original intent of the Sabbath were observed, no one—not even a visiting foreigner—could be asked to give up the privilege of an uninterrupted, restful day. The poorest person in town could not be ordered around by a wealthy tycoon, demanding all the services money can buy. The Sab-bath was blessed so that all people can participate in its blessing, observing the rest that celebrates the beauty of creation. Indeed there is a forceful reminder that all of creation is involved in the meaning of the Sabbath, for even the cattle are to be given a day of rest.

Our first Sabbath in Israel was a beautiful day in Meron, a delightful town in northern Israel where the great majority of the people were Orthodox Jews. The Sab-bath began officially when the first star appeared in the sky on Friday evening. Families walked together to worship at their synagogue which was within walking distance of everyone in the community. The serenity of that sunny Sabbath added a sense of blessing to the day. For us it was a first-hand experience of the Jewish Sabbath: a whole community enjoying the shared re-freshment of restful quiet. Small family groups or friends took leisurely walks along the simple town roads. The perfect peace was enhanced by the absence of cars, for their use was forbidden on the Sabbath. We enjoyed our own experience of an unrushed Sabbath walk in the lovely nearby countryside. We were intrigued by the many flowers—excitingly new to us—growing along the roadside. A small, well-kept garden hugged each home in Meron. The songs of the birds affirmed, rather than interrupted, the meaning of the Sabbath.

Even now, years later, I am reminded of that lovely day, as I read a sentence in Moltmann's book describing the Sabbath: "The ecological day of rest should be a day without pollution of the environment—a day when we leave our cars at home, so that nature too can celebrate its sabbath."[9] And I smile with happy memories of that day when I read that the Sabbath blessing includes sojourners:

> Remember the Sabbath day, to keep it holy. Six days you shall labor and do all your work, but the seventh day is the Sabbath of the Lord your God. In it you shall do no work: you, nor your son, nor your daughter, nor your manservant, nor your maidservant, nor your cattle, nor your stranger who is within your gates.
>
> Ex. 20:8-10

Jesus' words remind us that indeed the Sabbath is a gift from the Creator, who understands our need for rest: "The Sabbath was made for man, and not man for the Sabbath" (Mark 2:27).

But the Sabbath was meant for all creation! Why has man robbed creation of its God-given blessing of the Sabbath rest?

Only as we recognize the rate at which our whole environment is being polluted, do we realize that all creation needs rest. Only as we admit the need for cleansing and renewal of our own inner environment, do we appreciate the rest the Creator planned and gave us with His blessing!

The declaration of a Sabbath for the land affirms the Creator's concern for the preservation of the earth. Very early in her history, Israel recognized that the land needed rest and renewal. Just as the seventh day of each week was a day of rest, remembering the Creator's rest as He celebrated the greatness of creation, so every seventh year was a year of rest for the land, practiced as a recognition of the environment and His continuing concern for its preservation (Lev. 25:1–7).

The year of Jubilee was the ultimate celebration. After seven Sabbaths for the land, (that is, the fiftieth year) the land was returned to the family it had been assigned to when the twelve tribes first entered the Promised Land. Originally the land was distributed according to the biblical procedure detailing how much land each family in each tribe would receive and where it would be located. The land was never sold nor new land purchased, for all the land belonged to God. Each generation inherited the stewardship of the land with serious, continuing spiritual significance. Each Sabbath year no crops were planted on it; the land remained fallow in renewing rest.

These guidelines for a Sabbath for the land were given to Moses before the Israelites entered the Promised Land, and are an amazing example of environmental protection. The twenty-fifth chapter of Leviticus describes, at considerable length, the meaning of the Creator's message for a Sabbath for the land:

> When you come into the land which I give, the land shall keep a Sabbath to the Lord . . . In the seventh year you shall not sow your field or prune your vineyard. It shall be a year of solemn rest for the land. And you shall count seven times seven years . . .and on the day of atonement you shall hallow the fiftieth year and proclaim liberty throughout the land . . . . when each of you shall return to his property and each of you shall return to his land . . .You shall not wrong one another, but you will fear your God; for I am the Lord your God . . .You will keep my ordinances . . . so you will dwell in the land securely. The land shall not be sold in perpetuity, for the land is mine, for you are strangers and sojourners with me . . . You shall grant a redemption of the land.
>
> Lev. 25:2–24

This theology of the land played a central role in Jewish tradition. The Sabbath of the land was a practical, profound expression that the land really belonged to God. He gave man stewardship of the land and its abundant harvest, and guidelines for its care. Responsibility to God meant renewing the land in Sabbatical rest. Responsibility to one's neighbor meant integrity:

"You shall not oppress one another, but you shall fear
your God; for I am the Lord your God . . . . So you will
dwell in the land in safety . . . .The land will yield its
fruit, and you will eat your fill, and dwell there in safety"
(Lev. 25: 17–19).

The people's inner environments influenced their
care of the land, their attitudes toward God and their
neighbors, and their recognition that the ultimate owner
of the land was the Creator. No self-centered arrogance or selfish purchasing was to characterize their
attitudes or actions in relation to the land. The people
were told that when they came to "the land which the
Lord your God is giving you" they were to witness to
each other, to their children, and to the warring world
around them that the land belonged to the God who
said: "You shall love the Lord your God with all your
heart, with all your soul, and with all your might" and
"you shall love . . . . your neighbor as yourself"
(Deut.6:5; Luke10:27).   Indeed, recognition of this
greatest Law, given in the Old Testament and affirmed
in the New Testament, was to be passed from generation to generation, witnessing to the power in this Law
to protect the environment.

The symbols and celebrations in Judeo-Christian
traditions are rich in the imagery of faith. The Jubilee
year, following seven times seven Sabbatical years, was
a special year celebrating the Creator's care. The land
must be allowed to rest, and also must be returned to
the descendants of its original owners.

How meaningful that this event was to take place on the Day of Atonement (Lev. 25:9). What a complicated mixture of psychological actions and reactions must have occurred when the time came to give up land held for years. How appropriate that this happened in the context of the Day of Atonement when a sacrifice was offered for sin (self-centeredness), and when forgiveness was sought from God. The Sabbath of the land began with the symbols of the Day of Atonement: God's cleansing, forgiveness and renewal of man's inner environment, and then His blessing and renewal of the whole environment of the land!

Long before the phrase "pollution of the environment" became as commonplace as it is today, the concept of pollution was taught faithfully in the Scriptures. Numerous references are made about pollutions that must be avoided: in the land, the food, the house of the Lord, the table of the Lord, the Sabbath, and the human heart. The emphasis is not only on the need for cleansing, but also on the desire of a forgiving God to give cleansing.

If we are to effectively deal with pollution—wherever it occurs—we must recognize its cause and learn how to accomplish cleansing and renewal. This is especially important today, as we face ever increasing environmental problems.

The Eden story offers glimpses into the basic relationship between man's spirit and his attitude toward creation. In order to deal with environmental pollution of the planet, we must recognize the destructive effects of self-interest and self-centeredness in the inner environment of each person. We must face the basic problem: the need for renewal of man's spirit. The Sabbath is a continuing reminder that the Creator seeks to give rest and renewal to each person and to the whole planet.

Questions:

Why was the creation of *rest* an important part of the Genesis account? Why was a *special* blessing placed on the Day of Rest?

Why is rest itself so creative in our lives?

How essential was the gift of Sabbath rest for:
(a) the land and its fruitfulness?
(b) all creatures whose life depends on land, sea and air?
(c) all people in the midst of toil and stress?

What are we asked to *"remember"* in the ten commandments? How can *remembering* and *rest* increase our enjoyment in creation?

Chapter Six

———— • ————

The Renewal Offered

———— • ————

I will cleanse you. . . . I will give you a new
heart and put a new spirit within you.
—Ezekiel 36:25–26

The offer of renewed life is a basic theme in the Judeo-Christian Scriptures. From Eden onward, the Creator has sought to redeem and renew the spirit of man.

Perhaps nowhere is this more strikingly illustrated than in the dramatic vision of the prophet Ezekiel during a time of particular discouragement for the nation of Israel. In the midst of a valley filled with dry bones, Ezekiel heard God explain: "these bones are the whole house of Israel. They indeed say, 'Our bones are dry. Our hope is lost, and we ourselves are cut off!'"(Ez. 37:11). Yet the Great Questioner asked the prophet, "Son of man, can these bones live?" (Ez. 37:3). And in a mighty spectacular foreshadowing of resurrection power, the amazed Ezekiel saw the Spirit of God bring the bones together, knit them with sinew and flesh, and finally breathe new life into them. Filled with life again, the dry bones began to dance! The prophet recognized God's message of hope for His discouraged people: "I will give you a new heart and put a new spirit within you. . . . Then you shall dwell in the land that I gave to your fathers; you shall be My people, and I will be your God" (Ez. 36:26-28).

But who believed this good news?

Even after this great display of God's renewing Spirit, the people seemed unimpressed. No one truly believed God's awesome deed in the valley. By parable and preaching Ezekiel tried to help them understand. But they continued to live as "dry bones" and declined the Creator's invitation to be restored and to join the dance.

The Great Questioner asked them an amazing question: "Why should you die? For I have no pleasure in the death of one who dies. . . therefore turn and live" (Ez. 18:31-32).

Ezekiel reminds them that God takes the initiative in redemption and renewal of both man and beast. If only they could understand God's promise in the 34th Chapter of Ezekiel:

> I Myself will search for My sheep and seek them out. . . . I
> will seek what was lost and bring back what was driven away,
> bind up the broken and strengthen what was sick . . . . I will
> make a covenant of peace with them . . . .I will make them
> and the places all around My hill a blessing; and I will cause
> showers to come down in their season; there shall be

showers of blessing. Then the trees of the field shall yield
their fruit, and the earth shall yield her increase.
Ez. 34:11-27

The offer of cleansing and renewal from the toxic
effects of self-centeredness is the great story of redemption. Again and again the Bible describes the path to
a complete inner cleansing with words such as *repen-
tance, redemption, atonement* and *forgiveness*. And
many times the cleansing of the inner environment is
linked with the healing of the land.

At the historic dedication of Solomon's great temple,
God gave this message to the king as he prayed: "If
My people who are called by My name will humble
themselves, and pray and seek My face, and turn from
their wicked ways, then I will hear from heaven, and
will forgive their sin and heal their land" (2 Chron.7:14).

Over and over the Bible refers to "atonement." This
word is the opposite of "cover-up." It means that
cleansing from sin is accomplished by its removal.
Atonement acknowledges that wrong-doing has destroyed the harmony in relationships, and it provides
the means of purification or "at-one-ment." The Old
Testament is rich with the joy of atonement and cleansing—the renewal of life in the inner environment. How
often the psalmist prayed for cleansing and then praised
God when he received it.

The Incarnation—the Christmas story—is the fulfillment of that great prophecy. Christ came to the
Garden Planet. He came to live in His creation as the

second Adam. He came to redeem creation from the first Adam's sin. He became like us so that we could be renewed in His likeness. In the midst of His creation, the second Adam would live among us as a man who must respond fully to the laws of God in the midst of the problems on the Garden Planet.

As a boy growing up in a devout Jewish home, Jesus probably spent many hours studying the Torah. Describing Christ's education, David Flusser, Professor of Religious History at Hebrew University in Jerusalem, said: "Viewing Jesus' sayings against the background of contemporary Jewish learning, it is easy to observe that Jesus was far from uneducated. He was perfectly at home in holy scripture, and in oral tradition, and knew how to apply this scholarly heritage." Flusser regarded Jesus' Jewish education to be superior even to that of the apostle Paul.[1]

Well known to Jesus would be the Scriptures' teachings about the pollution of the heart. The Gospel of Luke conveys the eagerness of that young Jewish boy's thirst for God's law as he "increased in wisdom and stature" (Luke 2:52). At the age of twelve He and His family traveled from the rural town of Nazareth to the temple in Jerusalem. That was the appropriate time for His bar mitzvah, when He would be questioned about His understanding of the Law. As he lingered in the temple in dialogue with the Jewish scholars, we are told of their reaction to Him: "all who heard him were astonished at His understanding and answers" (Luke 2:47).

Jesus knew well the meaning of the sacrificial lamb for the atonement of sin. His understanding of the Scriptures gave grim portent to John's greeting when Jesus presented Himself at the Jordan for baptism: "Behold! The Lamb of God who takes away the sin of the world!" (John 1:29).

The Gospel carefully identifies the Person who is the Lamb of God with the person and work of the Creator. There is a fascinating parallel between the Genesis account of creation and the first chapter of John's Gospel. Both books open with the words, "In the beginning." Both discuss creation first. The wonder of creation is first conveyed in light which triumphed over darkness. "Let there be light," was the first creative command in Genesis (Gen 1:3). And Christ was proclaimed by John as the Light who "shines in the darkness":

> In the beginning was the Word, and the Word was with God, and the Word was God.
> He was in the beginning with God.
> All things were made through Him, and without Him nothing was made that was made.
> In Him was life, and the life was the light of men.
> And the light shines in the darkness, and the darkness did not comprehend it.
> There was a man sent from God, whose name was John.
> This man came for a witness, to bear witness of the Light, that all through him might believe.
> He was not that Light, but was sent to bear witness of that Light.
> That was the true Light which gives light to every man who comes into the world.

He was in the world, and the world was made through
Him, and the world did not know Him.
John 1:1-10

Today, technical laboratories around the world are
conducting advanced research to identify the exact role
of light in the beginning of the universe.

The wonder of creation was effectively displayed in a
ninety-minute science program televised in 1985 entitled
"The Creation of the Universe." Host Timothy Ferris
opened the program saying, "To know the atom it seems
we must know the universe . . . .the search for simplicity
is bringing science face to face with the ancient enigma of
creation."[2] The program attracted an exceptionally large
audience; in fact, the public's written response was so great
that the office of Public Television Publications required
months to fill all the requests for copies of the transcript.
The program's subtitle read: "The innermost reaches of
the atom and the outermost reaches of the universe are
surprisingly linked in the search for the evidence about
conditions at the instant of creation."[3] With rich clarity
and deep conviction, Ferris communicated what modern
science affirms: light had a basic, primal role in creation.

The opening chapter of Genesis describes God's
continuing work after His initial words, "Let there be
light." He then created the entire environment of the
universe. John's opening chapter identifies Christ as
the Word of God who shared in the creation. He
Himself is the Light that went forth to give life to the
inner environment!

The message of the Gospel is that God seeks to cleanse all creation, with its two environments, from the contaminating influence of man's self-centeredness and self-interest. But how can these pollutants be removed? When an area is contaminated by radioactivity, specific means must be taken to cleanse it completely, not cover it cosmetically. (Amen!) As we saw previously, this thorough cleansing is beyond the test of man's natural eyesight. It must be verified by an authentic test for purity. And so it is with our inner environment. Christ spoke about the authentic test for His cleansing of our hearts: "The Spirit Himself bears witness with our spirit that we are children of God" (Rom. 8:16). The blood of Christ cleanses us from all sin.

During His life on the Garden Planet, Christ continually identified with His creation. A star moved across the sky to welcome His birth. His earliest crib was with the cattle. The message of His advent was sung in the heavens and heard in the fields. He grew up in Nazareth of Galilee, the agricultural area whose simple country accent made Peter the object of scorn in the courtyard of Caiaphas.

Jesus filled His stories and sermons with wonderful illustrations from the creation He loved. In what came to be known as the "Sermon on the Mount" (Matt. 5:1-7:29), He spoke of God's care for the birds of the air, the common grass, and the lilies of the field. He began with a strange blessing: He blessed those who recognize the poverty of their own spirit. Indeed, the kingdom of God is for those who recognize the deep need of their inner environment.

Multitudes listened eagerly to Jesus as He preached about the kingdom within. Many among them knew the words of the psalmist exalting the glory of God in the heavens:

> How excellent is Your name in all the earth,
> You who set Your glory above the heavens! . . .
> When I consider Your heavens, the work of Your fingers,
> The moon and the stars, which You have ordained,
> What is man that You are mindful of Him . . ?
>
> Psalm 8:1–4

Then Jesus asked them to really consider the beauty and detailed design in the lilies growing around them. By Jesus' standards, Solomon in all his costly robes could not compare with the lilies which bore the continuing beauty of the Creator's care. We take the lily so for granted, but if we examine the details of its cellular arrangement under a microscope, it is as awesome in its minute detail as the stars of heaven in their grandeur and magnitude. Jesus loved the flowers like the gardener who tends them!

Even the grass of the field provided Jesus with a rich illustration of the Creator's care. Grass is the most common ground cover and it helps preserve the topsoil of the earth. Any botanist can affirm the vital role of grass in the environmental system of our planet. Ask a botanist to describe the unique design built into some grasses which allows them to stay green and growing when they are repeatedly grazed by cattle and sheep. In Jesus' day the poor used dried grass cuttings as their source of fuel. Jesus reminds us that even grass, the most common of all plant life, illustrates the continuing care of God: "Now if God so clothes the grass of the field . . .will He not much more clothe you, O you of little faith?" (Matt. 6:30).

Again, in that wonderful outdoor sermon, Jesus asked the listening crowd to consider the birds of the air. Perhaps He raised His hand to point out the graceful wonder of the soaring birds whose flight seemed so effortless. A.H. McNeile says, "The birds are an example not of idleness, but of freedom from anxiety."[4] And the heavenly Father, who designed their form and flight, would take care to feed His creatures. His radar screen of compassion catches even the fall of the sparrow!

Jesus proclaimed that the birds of the air and the lilies of the field are visual aids in our understanding of God's character. If God provides so abundantly in the environmental balance of life, will He not care even more for you, in whose inner environment His kingdom resides? Thus Jesus reiterates a basic theme throughout the Sermon on the Mount: the first priority of His disciples must be the kingdom of God that is within. "But seek first the kingdom of God and His righteousness, and all these things shall be added to you" (Matt. 6:33). The true growth of the soul comes through a "ministry of the interior," hidden in the inner environment.

Jesus warned us that publicity-seeking can seriously endanger our inner environment. Modern medical experts remind us of health hazards to our bodies from long exposure to sunlight. Jesus speaks of the greater danger to our souls from basking in the glare of public approval. The three illustrations which Jesus gave are well related to the Greatest Law. If we claim to love God with all our heart, we damage our prayer life by parading it before others. (This certainly is not a statement to discourage prayer *with* others, as Jesus promised to be with them when they met together in prayer.) But true prayer is *before* God—with the one desire to please and to praise Him.

If we claim to love our neighbor, we will give him our gifts of charity privately in the most gentle way possible, seeking to preserve his dignity. We will seek our neighbor's good, not our glory.

If we understand what it means to accept and love the person we are in God's image in the light of God's love, we will discipline ourselves (including fasting) not seeking to magnify our public image but to purify our inner environment. How typical of God, who hides the great power of energy in the unseen atom and the greatest pattern of life in the tiny gene, to treasure what is hidden in the heart!

Jesus concluded His sermon with an illustration about house-building and soil erosion. Two men were each building a house. The difference between the houses was not in their appearance, size, or design. The basic difference began with each builder's understanding of the environment and the quality of the foundation needed to withstand rain, floods, winds, and soil erosion. Both houses looked strong until they were tested by environmental conditions. The wise man understood the needs and chose to build his house on a sturdy rock that would not erode or shift. The foundation might be hidden, but the whole house depended on the strength of that hidden foundation. The foolish man ignored the environmental problems and found it quicker and cheaper to build on the sand. After all, he figured, how many people are going to look at my foundation? He chose the easier way.

"Now everyone who hears these sayings of Mine, and does not do them," Jesus concluded, "will be like a foolish man who built his house on the sand: and the rain descended, the floods, came, and the winds blew and beat on that house; and it fell. And great was its fall " (Matt. 7:26-27).

In all His stories, the Great Storyteller expressed with authority the good news of God's compassion. There was a freshness of the out-of-doors in His words, and the people heard Him gladly because He illustrated truth with experiences they understood: searching diligently for a lost coin, or admitting to a neighbor you didn't have enough food in the house to feed an unexpected visitor, or mending clothes. When did you last hear a sermon on mending clothes?

He spoke of farmers, weeds, soil samples, sheep, barn-building, lazy servants, and unkind masters. He often spoke of vines, pruning, and vinekeepers, favorite illustrations because in Jewish Scripture, the vine was the symbol of God's work in nurturing His people. The prophet Jeremiah told the parable of a vineyard planted by God and given special care for its preservation. But His care seemed to be wasted; later the Creator asked: "Yet I had planted you a noble vine, a seed of highest quality. How then have you turned before Me into the degenerate plant of an alien vine?" (Jer. 2:21).

The Great Questioner, by parables and stories, asks us to meditate on the hidden reasons for the changes in our lives, and consider His offer of renewal: "I will cleanse you . . . . I will give you a new heart" (Ez. 36:25-26).

Questions:

Compare the story of creation in the first chapter of Genesis with the first chapter of the Gospel of John. How basic is *light* in both?

How does the gospel of John describe Christ's role in creation? What insight does this give to the Creator's words: "Let *us* make man in our *own* image"?

How is the inner environment presented in both Genesis and John?

What emphasis is given in Christ's work in the creation of the inner environment?

How does Christ's redeeming care of the inner environment affect our whole attitude to the Garden Planet?

Chapter Seven

—————— · ——————

The Great Storyteller

—————— · ——————

No man ever spoke like this Man!
—John 7:46 NIV

Storytelling has had an important place in the heritage of every country and culture. Like heirlooms of the heart, favorite stories are passed from generation to generation to enrich both heart and mind with the model of the hero's character revealed in a crisis. Well-told stories of the past give a living sense of history.

Years ago, my husband and I were privileged to hear an old sea captain tell authentic stories of Maine's distant past. The rugged mariner had perfected the ancient art of telling stories. He had sailed the windswept coasts and he shared with us the wild, unwritten stories of olden days. The stories were so vivid a listener could feel the sting of the storm and taste the briny spray of the sea.

The old storyteller trimmed his words as masterfully as he trimmed his sails, leaving no words rattling loosely in the wind. The actions and reactions of seafaring life demanded a short cargo of words. The mariner's face and his expression-filled eyes told us he was reliving these strange experiences, granting just a glimpse of their reality to his rapt audience. The sea was a part of every story, the wonder varied with the amazing character people revealed in the crises of life's storms.

Like the sea captain's stories, the best tales are well-trimmed to sail a straight, clear course toward a meaningful goal. People of all ages love a well-told story, especially if it touches them where they are, and then takes them beyond it to a place they could only dream about.

The Bible is filled with stories of the drama of life in all its diversity. Children love to hear the exciting adventures of those who believed in God, and followed His call. As we grow older, we realize that the call of God is something like the call of the sea—the one who hears it is the one who has an understanding of the nature of the Caller. And any child deprived of the time-tested wonder of Bible stories has missed something of the most exciting story in the world: the power of a great God who made this Garden Planet, loves every person in this Garden, and desires to remove all pollution that destroys the real beauty of the inner and outer environment.

Throughout the busy years of His earthly ministry, Jesus Christ became famous as the Man who told amazing stories. No one touched more lives than the outdoor Storyteller who loved to teach by the Sea of Galilee.

Because He changed so many lives with His stories, millions of people have found the story of His life, death, and resurrection to be the greatest story ever told. Thousands of language scholars have spent their lives translating the story of His life and His message into other languages, so that all around this Garden Planet people might read it in their own language. The story of Jesus Christ has been translated into more languages than any other book in the world. Now that story can be read in more than two thousand different languages. Today His name is recognized all around the planet!

The common people heard this Storyteller gladly. Professional storytellers were not unusual—some told fascinating tales to earn money, others were traveling fable-makers who sought power or political gain. The people learned by experience not to trust every itinerant preacher. They'd heard a lot of tall tales. But what a difference there was when Jesus of Nazareth spoke!

Over the centuries people from every walk of life have searched for the real identity of the Great Storyteller. During His lifetime, no one could explain the strange, awesome beauty of His life and of His message. Some people said He was a king, but He had lived His life so simply. He had an inner stillness that helped people see inside themselves. He often spoke of a joy that this world can neither give nor take away. His life abounded in this mysterious joy. Was he prophet or charlatan, a mere man or the Son of God? C. S. Lewis, Professor of Medieval and Renaissance English Literature at Cambridge University, spent many hours scrutinizing the Gospel records. Applying the critical analysis of his own discipline, he affirmed: "I was by now too experienced in literary criticism to regard the Gospels as myths. They had not the mythical taste. . . . Here and here only in all time. . . . the Word [became] flesh; God [became] Man."[1]

The exact time of His birth is unknown, yet every international document circulated throughout the world today bears a date recognizing His birth as the center of time in history. In all of human history no one has ever lived more simply, and changed the world more profoundly.

Common people, though untrained in the methods used by scholars like Lewis, have an uncanny way of recognizing counterfeit Christianity. In Jesus' day, those who had listened to so many other self-proclaimed preachers said with awe, "No man ever spoke like this Man!" (John 7:46). They loved the way He spoke on their level and told stories about things that were real in their lives. And the most wonderful parts of all were his enthusiastic stories about the character of the loving God.

The real hero in all of Jesus' stories was the Father. To know God was the greatest joy in life. He said that the heart of the Gospel was found in the character of God. He talked simply about His Father who loved purity and hated pollution, a God who gladly gave love and joy to all who admitted their need and turned to Him for renewal.

But who ever talked about the joy of God?

It was a new experience for Jesus' listeners to hear about a joyful God. They were accustomed to hearing about a stern, distant deity far removed from their daily lives as they endured the hard realities of Roman domination. Jesus assured them that He understood and wanted to share with them the meaning of the Gospel.

The Great Storyteller emphasized that His primary reason for coming was to reveal God's deep care for His creation and His joy in redeeming the lost. God's ultimate joy and purpose was to conquer the pollution that had spoiled the entire physical environment of the world and the inner environment in each heart. The Gospel promised a full and final answer to the ecological pollution of the universe: a new heaven and a new earth bursting with shared joy of its complete renewal (Rev.21:1).

Jesus delighted in illustrating the joy of God. When we read His parables and tales we often focus on the problems and miss the central theme He wants to share with us: the *joy* of God!

One well-remembered story is of a caring shepherd who lost one of his hundred sheep (Luke 15:3-6). Jesus opened with a question:

"What man of you, having a hundred sheep, if he loses one of them, does not leave the ninety-nine in the wilderness, and go after the one which is lost until he finds it?" (v. 4)

Jesus glanced around the group of listeners. Their nods of recognition assured Him they understood the problem of losing sheep. He drew on their personal experience of joy in finding their own sheep and the desire to share that joy with others. They smiled knowingly as He described the happy celebration with friends and neighbors when the shepherd returned home carrying the lost sheep on his shoulders. Then He amazed them by saying that God is like that shepherd who celebrates when He redeems a lost sinner. The Caring Creator wants to share His joyful celebration with us!

Could there be such good news as this?

Were we really created that we might share the joy of God in His Creation and Redemption?

Just think, He is One who cares and says: "Rejoice with me!" (Luke 15:6).

A favorite parable of millions of people around the world is about the prodigal son: a family study about a loving father of two sons with very different attitudes and dispositions (Luke 15:11-32). The story is about God's joy and how one son found it and the other missed it.

The rebellious younger son demanded his independence, his inheritance, and his right to leave home. He filled his life with every indulgence that money and freedom made possible, until he exhausted his resources. He ended up a homeless person who could only get work feeding pigs.

Smelling the filth of the pig pen, he finally "came to himself" and reflected on his condition and all that he had given up through his self-centeredness (Luke 15:17). He realized he had squandered his birthright.

He knew he was no longer worthy to live as a son in his father's home. He would now consider it a privilege just to be a servant there! He set out for home, rehearsing his awkward confession.

The hero of this family story is the father—ever watching the road, never giving up hope that someday his rebellious son would return home.

One day, as he stood gazing across the fields, a solitary figure came into view. There was a subtle familiarity about the young man, and suddenly the father recognized his younger son! Even though he was thin, weary, barefoot, and tattered, there was no mistaking him.

With tremendous joy, the father ran down the road to meet him, took him in his lonely arms and kissed him. Overcome by his father's love, the son stammered: "Father, I have sinned against heaven and in your sight, and am no longer worthy to be called your son" (Luke 15:21).

But the joy of the father was beyond words. He delighted in forgiving those who wanted to make things right. His greatest joy was in redeeming what had been lost. He told the servants to bring the best robe, sandals, and the family signet ring to assure his son how gladly and fully he was welcomed back into the family. "And bring the fatted calf here and kill it, and let us eat and be merry; for this my son was dead, and is alive again; he was lost, and is found" (Luke 15:23–24).

And indeed they did make merry, throwing a party that included a delicious feast and music and dancing. The great joy of the father filled the homecoming.

But his older son did not understand or share his father's joy. Self-centered and self-satisfied, he refused to come in to the party.

Again the father went out to meet a son. But with obvious jealousy and a thankless heart, the older son said: "Lo these many years I have been serving you. . . . yet you never gave me a young goat, that I might make merry with my friends. But as soon this son of yours came, who has devoured your livelihood with harlots, you kill the fatted calf for him" (Luke 15:29–30).

His father caringly replied, "Son, you are always with me, and all that I have is yours. It was right that we should make merry and be glad, for your brother was dead and is alive again, and was lost and is found" (Luke 15:31–32).

The older brother had stayed close to his father physically, but was far from understanding his father's heart. Focused on himself, he could neither see nor appreciate the flood of relief and joy his father felt at regaining a "dead" son. He thought of his father in terms of duty and routine rather than love and relationship.

A generous, loving father went out to greet two sons, but only one son would return with him. The younger son learned the joy of reclaimed life. He appreciated his father's forgiveness and loving welcome, while the older brother's heart was blocked by bitterness and resentment. Only those who understood the heart of the father could appreciate the joyous music of the homecoming party.

Music is a wonderful feature of God's celebrations and the joyful response of His creation throughout the Scripture. God Himself is pictured as singing in Zephaniah 3:17: "The Lord your God in your midst. . . . He will rejoice over you with gladness, He will quiet you in His love, He will rejoice over you with singing." Moses called God his song in Exodus 15:2: "The Lord is my strength and song."

But perhaps the psalms of David most fully develop the relationship of music and singing to the joy of the Lord. As a young shepherd, David practiced the music of the lyre in the solitary beauty of God's green pastures. It might seem only the sheep heard his happy music played in the full harmony that comes when heart, head, and hand are touched by the joy of God. But that's not true, for David said, "I will sing to the Lord" (Ps. 13:6).

I wonder if David watched the reactions of his sheep to his varied kinds of music. Did he know which music quieted their restless fears after a lion or bear attacked the flock? Was it in just such situations that David learned to play the kind of music that soothed the frenzied, fearful mind of King Saul back to sanity?

David also knew the quiet peace of still waters, and the music that creation itself made in response to the Creator:

> The hills are clothed with gladness,
> The meadows are covered with flocks

The Valleys are mantled with grain;
They shout for joy and sing.

Ps. 65:12-13 NIV

The theme of so many biblical stories—that God
Himself gives the song of joy—must have been very real
to Christ. For He shared this song of joy with His
disciples after their last Passover meal together. The
disciples joined Him in a hymn of praise before they left
for Gethsemane.

Throughout the evening He had tried to comfort the
disciples even though it was He who would face the
cross. He knew they were deeply concerned and
troubled, so He spoke to them of a joy that the world
could not take away: "These things have I spoken to
you that My joy may remain in you, and your joy may
be full. . . . you now have sorrow, but I will see you
again and your heart will rejoice, and your joy no one
will take from you. . . . Ask, and you will receive, that
your joy may be full" (John 15:11; 16:22–24). Remembering that His disciples would soon see one of
their own betray Him and another deny Him before His
crucifixion, He prayed for them "that they may have
My joy fulfilled in themselves" (John 17:13).

It is amazing how many times the Great Storyteller
talked about joy. Perhaps one of the most important keys
to appreciating a person's character is to discover what
brings him the most joy. Christ surprised a lot of people
by talking about the joy of God and the God of joy.

Jesus said that He came to bring good news from God. Soon after His baptism He returned to his home town of Nazareth. On the Sabbath He went to the synagogue as was His custom. He was recognized as a member of the community and invited to speak. Handed the scroll of the prophet Isaiah, He opened it and read:

> The Spirit of the Lord God is upon Me,
> Because He has anointed me
> To preach the gospel to the poor.
> He has sent me to heal the brokenhearted,
> To preach deliverance to the captives
> And recovery of sight to the blind,
> To set at liberty those who are oppressed;
> To preach the acceptable year of the Lord.
>
> Luke 4:18-19

With quiet certainty Jesus added, "Today this scripture is fulfilled in your hearing" (Luke 4:21).

A chapter in Isaiah closes with verses of great joy:

> I will greatly rejoice in the Lord,
> My soul shall be joyful in my God. . . .
> For as the earth brings forth its bud,
> As the garden causes the things that are sown in it to
>   spring forth,
> So the Lord God will cause righteousness and praise to
> spring forth before all nations.
>
> Isa. 61:10-11

Indeed praise did spring forth before people of many nations as thousands gathered in Jerusalem on the day

of Pentecost and heard the message of the New Creation. But that message could only become reality after
the world-changing events of the Garden of Gethsemane and the Garden of the Resurrection. Christ knew
the painful paths He had to take on the Garden Planet,
and so for "the joy that was set before Him [redeeming
Creation] He endured the cross" (Heb. 12:2).

Questions:

How did Christ's stories help people understand His
messages?

What is your favorite story from the Great Storyteller?

Why?

What does the Parable of the Lost Sheep help us learn
about:
   (a) God's interest in each of us as individuals?
   (b) God's concern to help and heal what is lost?

What does the Parable of the Prodigal Son help us learn
about:
   (a) God's attitude to the choices we make?
   (b) God's attitude when we walk away from Him?
   (c) What does it mean to "come to yourself"?
           When does this happen?
   (d) What really brings us back to God?

———— · ————

Chapter Eight

The Beloved Garden

———— · ————

. . . there was a garden, which He and His disciples entered. And Judas, who betrayed Him, also knew the place; for Jesus often met there with His disciples.
—John 18:1-2

The Garden of Gethsemane was a favorite resting place for Jesus during the years of His public ministry. The peaceful beauty of the garden was only a short walk from the busy city, just beyond the little brook Kidron. During the demanding days of ministry in Jerusalem, Jesus was surrounded by the deep and urgent needs of humanity, so the garden was a place of refuge for Him.

But before Jesus ever began teaching others in His busy public ministry, He faced Satan in a time of testing in the wilderness, and He faced Himself as well. The isolation helped Him to see the needs of His own inner environment and to see how they could divert Him from

God's purposes. He knew how deeply self-centeredness influenced people's lives. In the wilderness He faced the strange, strong temptations to use the power He possessed as the Son of God to satisfy His own goals and needs. He could turn stones to bread to assuage His hunger. He could affirm that He was the Messiah by a dramatic act at the temple. Finally, he could gain the whole world, not by the Cross, but by surrendering to the evil one who had beguiled Adam, and who now promised Jesus, "All these things I will give You if You will fall down and worship me" (Matt. 4:9).

Jesus faced great challenges in His inner environment in the wilderness. Short cuts of self-centeredness can be a subtle temptation in the service of God, and the quiet stillness of the wilderness was the best place for Him to confront it. The soul sometimes has a fierce struggle with priorities.

In the midst of such temptations, Christ remembered the Word of God gave Him light and strength. Refusing the quick answers offered by Satan, Jesus chose to take the long path of obedience that led to the Garden of Gethsemane. "Though He was a son, yet He learned obedience by the things which He suffered" (Heb. 5:8).

When He made His commitment to center all His life and work in God, angels came to minister to Him in the wilderness. Then Jesus returned in the power of the Spirit to begin His ministry to the hidden needs of people.

His words were filled with the Spirit of God.

Thousands of searching people streamed miles along dusty roads to hear His message—a message that wrapped the great truths of God in simple stories that everyone could understand.

He taught in the temple, on crowded city streets, on grassy hillsides, and by the sea. His words burned like fire in the hearts and minds of the people. Suffering humanity pressed against Him as He responded to the piteous cries of the lepers and the tormented agonies of the demon-possessed. After stress-filled days like these, the serenity of the Garden of Gethsemane held a special blessing.

By common usage, the name of the Garden has become synonymous with "agony." But such an interpretation focuses on only one of Jesus' many visits to the Garden—His last. The actual translation of the name Gethsemane is "olive-press." The area abounded with olive trees, whose fruit produced much-needed olive oil.

The history of this area was as abundant as its trees. The Mount of Olives, close to Jerusalem's city wall, held a significant place in Jewish history and prophecy. A thousand years before Christ, King David had ascended this Mount, weeping as he went, for he realized his rule as king had been rejected by his people. And it would be this same road that Jesus would travel at the close of His ministry, weeping over the city of Jerusalem that was soon to reject Him. "If you had known . . . in this your day, the things that make for your peace" (Luke 19:41-42).

All four Gospels describe the importance of the Garden of Gethsemane in the life of Christ. Both Luke and John point out the frequency of Christ's visits to this favorite place, treasured for its undisturbed quiet. Here Jesus prayed to His Father; and here He would meet with a small group of His closest disciples, responding to questions they found difficult.

The twelve disciples understood the special meaning of this place for Jesus. When the conspiracy to capture Jesus was sealed, the priests authorized Judas to take armed men and arrest Him. Judas knew he would find Jesus in the gentle refuge of Gethsemane.

Gethsemane is central in the Garden Trilogy of the Bible. Each of the three gardens has its unique story. Together these stories develop the theme of the Creator's redeeming care for His whole creation. In Eden—the Garden of Beginnings—man walked with God in the beauty of creation, then walked away from God as he rebelled against His guidelines for the Garden. The thorns of self-interest changed all of Creation and all of mankind. In Gethsemane—the Garden of Cleansing—Christ prepared to pay the unbearably great cost of cleansing and renewing all creation. And finally, in the Garden of the Resurrection—the Garden of the New Creation—redemption was gloriously fulfilled and the future of the environment became bright with the promise of renewal.

Like a three-panelled altar triptych, whose two flanking panels can fold over the central picture, the Garden of Eden and the Garden of the Resurrection are better understood in relation to the central Garden of the Gospel: Gethsemane.

We would do well to meditate on the meaning of each of these gardens and consider the questions which the Great Questioner asks. We often spend so much time questioning God that we fail to hear the questions He is asking us.

In both Eden and Gethsemane, man is confronted with a choice: how will he respond to God's will? Significantly, the biblical story of man's beginnings reveals that man's first disobedience to God was expressed not in relation to other people, but in relation to God's authority in the environment He had created. In Eden, man chose to believe that the use of everything in the environment must bow to his desires and wishes. Gethsemane is the reversal of Eden. The first Adam, in Eden, represented all mankind in turning away from God and placing his own will at the center of his life. The second Adam, Christ, represented all mankind as He came to the Garden seeking a new beginning and communion with God, and seeking to put God's will at the center of His life. He prayed not only to *know* God's will, but to *do* God's will.

Christ brought His disciples with Him that they, too, might seek God in the Garden. But He went further into the Garden than anyone else. He prayed alone. He asked the disciples to pray, not for Him but for themselves: "Pray that you may not enter into temptation" (Luke 22:40).

But sleep drew the disciples more strongly than prayer. When Jesus returned to seek their fellowship He found them slumbering. Again He went into the Garden, alone. He was facing the greatest struggle of His life—to drink the cup of suffering, to accept the will of God. Again He returned and found them sleeping. He must have felt utterly alone in His agonizing conflict.

Even as He prayed, armed guards forced their way into the garden to arrest the Man who was seeking the will of God. They entered the garden with flaming torches and swords, polluting the quiet with noise, the fragrant air with the stench of burning pitch, and the attitude of prayer with words of hatred.

Perhaps no one in history more fully exemplifies the tragic effects of the knowledge of good and evil than Judas Iscariot. Christ had called him to become a disciple, and he had joined the intimate group that Jesus called friends (John 15:15). The disciples had trusted Judas enough to make him their treasurer. Their full confidence in Judas was evident at the Last Supper. That night Jesus revealed that He knew which one of the twelve—who were all present—would betray Him. Matthew tells us that the stunned, sorrowful disciples each asked: "Lord, is it I?" (Matt. 26:22). Each disciple sensed his own weakness. But Judas knew in his heart that he was the betrayer, and he was aware that Jesus knew it too.

The other disciples still didn't suspect Judas. After all, who can discern the hidden environment of another's soul? When Jesus told Judas, "What you do, do quickly," they thought He was telling him to go and buy what was needed for the feast or to give something to the poor (John 13:27-30). Deliberately, Judas joined the conspiracy to arrest Christ. He was well paid for his part in the betrayal. As they planned to take Jesus in the garden, Judas informed the guards that the person whom he kissed would be the one they should arrest. Perhaps nothing indicates more graphically the complete identification of Jesus with the common man than this: He was so indistinguishable from the ordinary fishermen who were His disciples that Judas had to identify Him by a specific sign—the deadly sign of a kiss.

Jesus had tried to prepare His disciples for what would happen in the lovely Garden of Gethsemane. If only they had glimpsed the ultimate meaning of the Cross! If they had understood the events to come, they too would have entered that Garden to pray. If only they had recognized the meaning of the cup He had offered as they celebrated the Passover! They slept while Jesus prayed alone, " O My Father, if it is possible, let this cup pass from Me; nevertheless, not as I will, but as You will" (Matt. 26:39).

The disciples didn't understand "the cup" of Gethsemane.

And I wonder if any of us has ever fully understood its meaning.

Together, in the upper room, they had shared the cup of the Passover celebrating God's covenant of historic deliverance from Egypt, the night when death passed over the Hebrew people in the midst of oppression. In this context Jesus gave new meaning to the cup as He thanked God and called it by a new name—the cup of the New Covenant. "This is My blood of the new covenant, which is shed for many for the remission of sins" (Matt. 26:28).

The wine which filled the cup of the Passover was the fruit of the vine—the symbol of God's work on earth, "For the vineyard of the Lord is His people" (Is. 5:7).

Then with a parable, Christ had shared something of the meaning of the Cup of the New Covenant, "I am the true vine, and My Father is the vinedresser" (John 15:1).

Jesus described the Father with a word which means vinedresser, or gardener, or one who labors with the soil. What a wonderful way to convey the Creator's care of His creation. In that redeeming care, the life of Christ—the true vine—is to be given in the cup of the New Covenant. Jesus offered His own life as the needed cleansing for the inner environment of mankind.

As they left for Gethsemane, the disciples had assured Him they would be faithful. Peter had insisted, "If I have to die with You, I will not deny You!" and all the others agreed (Mark 14:31). But Jesus knew the reality of their inner environment, and that they weren't nearly as strong as they thought.

Isn't that the final meaning of Gethsemane? It is the place where man's soul is stripped of all pretense, and the center of the will is revealed—to find if it is centered in self or in God.

What a contrast between the two Gardens! Unlike Adam who hid in the Garden, Jesus revealed Himself boldly. He went forward to meet His enemies saying, "Whom are you seeking?" (John 18:4).

Adam, in a history-changing act of selfishness, chose his own way; Jesus, in a history-changing act of self-denial, chose God's will. And the one who personified the Tree of the Knowledge of Good and Evil betrayed the One who personified the Tree of Life. But because God can cause all things to work together for good, that betrayal led to life for the whole world (Rom. 8:28).

Thorns—the sign of the pollution of the ground—were a warning to Adam as he left Eden. Those same thorns were made into a crown that Christ had to wear to the Cross. The pollution of the whole creation—the outer environment of the world and the inner environment of the spirit—was symbolized in the crown of thorns Christ wore. The pollution by man's self-interest was confronted and conquered by God's self-giving love.

Questions:

Why did Jesus go to Gethsemane so often? Why did He go there the last time?

In the Upper Room each disciple recognized that he was capable of denying Jesus. How well did each disciple understand his own inner environment? What helps each person recognize pollution in the inner environment?

In the Upper Room Christ spoke of the cost of cleansing the inner environment. How would cleansing of that environment be accomplished?

In what way is Gethsemane the reversal of Eden?

What did *the Cup* mean to Jesus? What are we asked to *remember* each time we take the cup of communion?

———— • ————

Chapter Nine

The Way to the Cross

———— • ————

*Behold, we are going up to Jerusalem, and the
Son of Man will be betrayed to the chief
priests and to the scribes; and they will con-
demn Him to death, and deliver Him to the
Gentiles to mock and to scourge and to crucify.*
—Matthew 20:18-19

*They clothed Him with purple; and they
twisted a crown of thorns, put it on His head,
and began to salute Him. . . and spat on Him;
and bowing the knee, they worshiped Him.
And when they had mocked Him, they took
the purple off Him, put His own clothes on
Him, and led Him out to crucify Him.*
—Mark 15:17-20

The Garden of Gethsemane was a crucial turning
point in the disciples' commitment to follow Christ
wherever He might lead them. There they saw that the
opposition to Jesus and His claims was becoming

violent. Until then He had been so popular. Crowds had gathered daily to hear Him in the temple. Just a few days earlier the multitudes had cast palm branches before Him as He rode into Jerusalem, shouting "Blessed is the King who comes in the name of the Lord!" (Luke 19:38)

But the Garden of Gethsemane saw the King turned into a shackled prisoner. With the same quiet dignity He had borne as He triumphantly rode into Jerusalem, the Great Questioner went forward to meet His enemies asking, "Have you come out, as against a robber, with swords and clubs? When I was with you daily in the temple, you did not try to seize Me. But this is your hour, and the power of darkness" (Luke 22:52–53).

The sense of the overwhelming power of darkness filled the Garden that once had been a place of peace and prayer. In the face of such evil, the disciples disbanded. They forsook Him and fled.

Bound as a common criminal, Jesus was forced to leave the Garden. He was stripped of His clothes and made a spectacle before a public court, wincing under the pain of violent lashing. He stood alone and faced the charges of blasphemy before the Jewish authorities, and was finally delivered to the Roman court which bore the seal of Caesar.

That Roman court represented the power of the Gentiles in their occupation of Jerusalem. Their ruling governor, Pilate, declared the final sentencing of Jesus. The key role of the Gentiles in the crucifixion of Jesus is seldom emphasized. Yet Jesus spoke directly about the shared responsibility of both Jews and Gentiles in His death. Matthew 20:18-19 reveals His understanding of the complicity of both: "Behold, we are going up to Jerusalem, and the Son of Man will be betrayed to the chief priests and to the scribes; and they will condemn Him to death, and deliver Him to the Gentiles to mock and to scourge and to crucify." It was as though all mankind was represented in the judgement passed on the Man who wore the crown of thorns.

The crowds in Jerusalem applauded the final sentence: "Let Him be crucified!" (Matt. 27:22) Exhausted in body and spirit, He began the wearying walk to Calvary carrying the wooden cross—wood that was once part of a living tree in the Garden Planet!

In the first century, crucifixion was the ultimate punishment. Professor Theodore Keim vividly described the stench and suffering of crucifixion in *Jesus of Nazara*.[1] Cicero stated that the tortures of crucifixion were so dehumanizing that no humane person would afflict it "even on a slave." Julius Caesar declared that captured pirates should be strangled before their naked bodies were degraded in public crucifixion. Keim concluded that "the Gospels have considerably spared us" the unspeakable horrors and humiliation of such a death.

Quoting ancient sources Keim reported: "Even among the Greeks and Romans there was, as a rule, no burial for the crucified. Sometimes, however, particularly on festival days, e.g., the birthdays of the emperors, the corpse was given to friends of the deceased."[2] The Jewish custom was different. The law ordained that the bodies of the hanged must be taken down at sunset, that the land might not be defiled (see Deut. 21:22-23).

Over the years the Christian church has glamorized the cross with a veneer of gold, and it is all too easy to forget what it really represents: the moral pollution of mankind in the decaying stench of Golgotha, the "Place of a Skull" (Matt 27:33).

The twenty-third chapter of Luke tells the poignant story of Jesus' journey to the place of His death. Knowing that He must suffer these things, Jesus began His long walk to Golgotha on the Via Dolorosa, the way of sorrow. Nowhere are the human limitations of His body more painfully evident than on that road. Exhausted by the all-night questioning and trial, the pain of the beatings, and the pricks of the thorns, He stumbled on, carrying His own cross. Luke tells us that a great multitude followed Him, many of them mourning for Him. Despite His agony, He was still sensitive to the pain that they, too, would face. He told them, "do not weep for Me, but weep for yourselves and for your children" (Luke 23:28).

Finally, His strength was completely spent. So as they led Him on, "they laid hold of a certain man, Simon a Cyrenian, who was coming from the country, and on him they laid the cross that he might bear it after Jesus" (Luke 23:26). Cyrene was the capital of Libya, and this African man was one of the compassionate strangers that ministered to the human needs of Christ in His final hours.

When they arrived at the Place of the Skull, He was nailed to the wood that once was a tree. Soldiers gambled for His garments at the foot of the cross. In naked agony, He wore the crown of thorns—Eden's symbol of pollution when man's self-interest spoiled the environment of creation. Jeers and blasphemy filled the air He painfully struggled to breathe.

In His loneliest hour He offered prayers from the psalms He had memorized in His youth. He acknowledged His humanity as He cried out in physical thirst for water, and in spiritual thirst for an answer from God: "Why have You forsaken Me?" (Matt. 27:46).

He found no answer in the cruel conduct of men. The final answer could only be in the character of God who sought to redeem the world He had created, even at great cost to Himself. But Jesus' tortured question was not His last utterance. His final words were a statement of faith, "Father, 'into Your hands I commend My spirit' " (Luke 23:46).

The strangeness of truth is seen in the reactions of three very different men to the dying Christ. The first was a common criminal who shared the date of his death sentence with Jesus. Somehow he had come to terms with his death, and even confessed he deserved to die. Crucifixion is a slow death. The three people crucified together at Golgotha had time for tortured thoughts and hate-filled conversation.

The Middle Man seemed to be talking to Someone invisible. Perhaps He was mad. After all, He *had* claimed to be the Christ. One of the criminals blasphemously taunted Him and crudely joked about His claims: "If you are the Christ, save Yourself and us" (Luke 23:39).

The other criminal had watched the Middle Man with growing amazement. In the midst of His pain He had been praying, with a Spirit unlike anything the confessing criminal had ever seen. The Middle Man cared about his mother. There was but one disciple standing at the foot of the cross beside His weeping mother. In His struggling, he asked this John to take care of Mary as if she were his own mother (see John 19:25-27). The cursing criminal and the confessing criminal reacted so differently to the Middle Man!

The confessing criminal, in the light of the cross, saw the darkness of his own inner environment in the light of the loving purity of the Middle Man. He rebuked the cursing criminal: "Do you not even fear God, seeing you are under the same condemnation? And we indeed justly, for we receive the due reward of our deeds; but this Man has done nothing wrong" (Luke 23:40-41). The confessing criminal saw the Light that both revealed and cleansed the inner environment of his soul. The Middle Man had shown him something of the holiness and judgment of God. The confessing criminal knew he must shout from his own polluted cross the message of God's evaluation of sin, and the redeeming love offered by the Middle Man.

What a strange story! The disciples, who had been with Him so long, and had so much "head knowledge" of His Gospel, had fled in fear. The confessing criminal was the only voice raised to ask a guilty world: "Do you not even fear God?" (Luke 23:40).

And then the forgiven criminal turned to the Middle Man. Of all humanity, he was the only one to say a kind word to the Savior while He suffered the lonely death of the contaminating cross. The confessing criminal recognized the King of Glory. "Then he said to Jesus, 'Lord, remember me when You come in Your kingdom.' And Jesus said to him: 'Assuredly, I say to you, today you will be with Me in Paradise' " (Luke 3:42–42).

Amazing grace from the cross had opened the path to Paradise. The forgiven thief entered the redeemed Eden!

The redeemed thief was the first of three men who brought gifts to the King. Each of the three bore public witness, so unexpectedly, to the worthiness of the King. Years ago, at His birth, wise men had come bringing gifts: "For we have seen His star in the East and have come to worship Him" (Matt. 2:2). And now in the darkest hour of the cross, three men from unexpected backgrounds–a thief, a scholar and a community leader—acknowledge that He *is* worthy and humbly offer Him the abiding gifts of faith, hope, and love.

A well-respected scholar, Nicodemus, was the second man. He had known Jesus much longer than the unnamed thief but he was not known as a follower of the Christ. Months ago he had called Jesus "Rabbi," the night he had gone to meet Him privately. He had been puzzled and perturbed by Jesus' teaching. He had said to Jesus: "We know that You are a teacher come from God; for no one can do these signs that You do unless God is with Him" (John 3:2). And Jesus had talked to him, carefully, about a cleansing of the inner environment that is so complete it is called "a new birth."

Jesus had pointed out to Nicodemus that the environment of the Spirit is of a different order than the environment of the flesh: "Most assuredly, I say to you, unless one is born of water and the Spirit, he cannot enter the kingdom of God. That which is born of the flesh is flesh, and that which is born of the Spirit is spirit" (John 3:5-6).

Nicodemus must have thought a great deal about that conversation. Some months later he heard that Jesus was teaching in Jerusalem. He went to the temple with a group of men sent by the priests to arrest Him. They must have been deeply moved by Jesus' powerful cry: "If anyone thirsts, let him come to me and drink. He who believes in Me, as the Scripture has said, out of his heart will flow rivers of living water" (John 7:37–38). They returned to the priests without Jesus and were asked why they had not brought Him. They could only answer, "No man ever spoke like this Man!" (John 7:46).

Was there really this kind of living water—springing up in one's heart like an artesian well of the spirit?

Nicodemus probably had a tremendous struggle with his own conscience. What did he believe and what would he do about it? He had thought the call of Christ too costly to follow. Yet the next time he made a public appearance in response to Christ's claims was at Calvary. The cross cast a new light on everything! God had so loved the world that He gave at all costs. Nicodemus counted costs differently now, in the light of Calvary. He decided that he must publicly declare his faith in Jesus Christ. This Pharisee whom Jesus respectfully called "a ruler in Israel" had come, bringing his gift of costly aloes and myrrh, to assist in the burial of Jesus.

But who could convince Pilate that the body should be released for burial?

The third man, Joseph of Arimathea.

He was a wealthy man whom Luke describes as "good and just" (Luke 23:50). He was a member of the council who "had not consented to their decision and deed" of Christ's arrest (Luke 23:51). He was "waiting for the Kingdom of God" (Luke 23:51). Joseph, a secret disciple, asked Pilate if he might take the body of Christ.

The gospel of Mark informs us that Pilate wondered if Jesus were really dead. Could His death by crucifixion possibly have been accomplished in three hours? Often criminals suffered agonizing torture that only ended in death after one or two days. Pilate summoned the centurion in charge of the crucifixion, and asked him to officially certify that Christ was dead (see Mark 15:44).

Only if proof of Christ's death were registered to Pilate's satisfaction could the body be released. This Man was so controversial! Only someone of undisputed trust could ever be given charge of the body. Pilate was convinced that no one could question the integrity of Joseph of Arimathea. After reviewing the facts, Pilate gave official permission. The body could be buried under Joseph's care.

Nicodemus, the scholar whom Jesus called "a teacher in Israel" (John 3:10) came forward with Joseph—risking his whole reputation. He gave the world his witness of faith in Christ. Together they would honor Christ in death, in the ritual of a Jewish burial. Together they prepared the body in the traditional Jewish burial custom. Reverently they placed is shrouded body in the Garden Tomb.

Scripture describes that tomb as new, one in which "no one had yet been laid" (John 19:41). This description was more meaningful to us after our visit to a number of ancient tombs in Israel which had been hewn out of rock about the time of Jesus. It was often customary for several generations to be buried in one tomb, in the real sense of being "gathered to their fathers" as expressed in the Torah (Judges 2:10). These ancient tombs were kept secure by a massive stone rolled in place against the entrance. Only by great strength could that stone be moved. In just such a tomb, the One who had worn the crown of thorns in death was buried, in a garden near the cross.

Questions

In what way was Gethsemane the turning point in the disciples' commitment to Jesus? Why?

How does the crown of thorns symbolize the pollution of both the inner environment of the person, and the whole environment of the Garden Planet?

Thinking about the message from the Gardens of Eden and Gethsemane, what meaning can be found in Christ's words from the cross: "It is finished"?

Who were the three unexpected men who witnessed to their faith in Christ at His Crucifixion? What do we know about the two men who buried Him in a Garden Tomb?

———— • ————

Chapter Ten

Garden Mysteries

———— • ————

To me . . . this grace was given, that I should . . . make all people see what is the fellowship of the mystery, which from the beginning of the ages has been hidden in God who created all things through Jesus Christ.
—Ephesians 3:8-9

Behold, I make all things new.
—Revelation 21:5

The third Garden in the Trilogy, unlike Eden and Gethsemane, bears no known name. It blooms quietly, hidden in history. The gospel story refers to it simply as "the garden near the cross." And it is the garden where all the life and hope of Christians spring forth. The events that took place in this garden are filled with mystery.   No greater mystery story has ever been written than the story of a Savior who redeems the world from its own pollution. Quietly, ever so gently, He returns again in the silence of a garden. Just as the quiet silence of the sea reflects the image of the sailboat anchored offshore, the deep silence of the Garden of the Resurrection reflects the character of God and His renewing power in the midst of His creation.

   To appreciate the richness of a mystery story it is always best to review the known facts. There had been a strangeness about the events of the days leading up to Jesus' death that disturbed the people of Jerusalem. Even at the trial, while Pilate was seated on the official judgment seat, he received a secret message from his wife: "Have nothing to do with that just Man, for I have suffered many things today in a dream because of Him" (Matt. 27:19). As Caesar's representative, Pilate had to deal with the impact of every event on this Roman-controlled society. Here was a Man who preached about the absolute claims of the kingdom of God. Each time He had spoken of the cross, He had also promised that He would rise again from the dead! He had publicly preached that the mystery of His identity would be answered by His resurrection three days after His death.

   The claims Christ made during His lifetime infuriated His enemies. He challenged the power structures of the world. "My kingdom is not of this world," He told Pilate with steely calm. Yet when Pilate challenged, "Are You a king, then?" He admitted, "You say rightly that I am a king" (John 18:36-37). It was with the greatest reluctance that Pilate had delivered Him to be crucified.

Because Roman custom left the bodies of the crucified to decay openly, it was expected that after dying a despised, dehumanizing death, Christ's body would be cast aside in the disgraceful treatment that customarily followed crucifixion.

What was different about this Man?

Something unexpected happened—an outstanding Jewish leader approached Pilate and requested the body of Christ for burial. The controversy and political pressures surrounding Jesus' trial, sentencing, and death made Pilate very cautious. Two facts had to be confirmed: that Jesus had been officially declared dead, and that the person to whom the body was released was a man of unquestioned integrity.

As we know from the previous chapter, Pilate wondered if Jesus were really dead. The centurion who was in charge of the crucifixion testified that one of the soldiers standing guard had made certain by thrusting a spear into Jesus' side. The body displayed no spasm of pain; in fact death had occurred so much earlier that the blood issuing from the site of the spear wound already showed post-mortem separation into cells and serum (blood and water).

Convinced of the certainty of Jesus' death and the integrity of Joseph of Arimathea, Pilate gave permission for the body of Jesus to be buried under Joseph's care.

With truth's strangeness beyond fiction, a rich man gave first place in his tomb to a poor Man who died among thieves. And many in Jerusalem asked: Just who was this Man they buried in the Garden? Over and over during His lifetime, people asked: "Who is this man?" (see Matt. 21:10). Jesus knew people questioned who He really was. One day, in the very cosmopolitan city of Caesarea Philippi (the northerly place most distant from Jerusalem in all His travels), He asked "Who do men say that I am?"(Mark 8:27) After a wide variety of answers He questioned His disciples: "But who do *you* say that I am?" (Mark 8:29)

And the mystery continued. Never a man ever lived like this! His crib had been borrowed from the cattle, and now His tomb was borrowed from a councillor. For years He had raised many questions in people's minds and consciences as He walked the streets of the crowded city, the dusty paths of the countryside, and the stony ways through the wilderness. He reminded those who claimed they would gladly follow Him: "Foxes have holes, and birds of the air have nests; but the Son of man has nowhere to lay His head" (Luke 9:58).

Continually this Man asked His disciples to see beyond the obvious—and the ordinary—and discern the hidden message of God. Throughout all His teaching, He stressed the hidden message of God. Throughout all His teaching, He stressed the importance of "keeping" (as in Eden) the inner environment of the heart: "Keep your heart with all diligence for out of it spring the issues of life" (Prov. 4:23).

This Man emphasized that it was in the inner environment of the heart that murder first began as hidden hatred. And adultery began in the inner environment as secret lust which flourished unrecognized by others. He preached that God cared deeply about the pollution of this inner environment. He saw through the impressive public image of false prophets who wore sheepskins to look like shepherds but their inner environment was the devious den of ravenous wolves.

This man said that God judged people by the hidden attitudes which motivated their actions, not by the public acclaim which produced those actions. He startled people by the great authority with which He spoke. Who really was this Man?

The mystery only continued to deepen during His lifetime. No one could explain the strange, awesome beauty of His life and of His message. Some people said He was a king. But He had lived His full life so simply. He said that what really mattered was not the riches of this world, but being "rich toward God," and that the most important thing in life was to know God. (Luke 12:21). Even though He was confronted at times by scorn, unbelief, and active hatred, a profound peace filled His whole life with such reflecting stillness that people saw the mirror image of their inner being when they came to Him for help. He often spoke of a joy that this world cannot give nor take away. His life abounded in this mysterious joy.

But that was all past.

Joseph had provided a new tomb in the Garden near the cross. The sad, strange burial procession had almost reached that tomb. The disciples who would have been expected to attend did not. Two unexpected men who had never publicly admitted their faith in Christ were in charge of the procession. How strange that the same disciples who had insisted they would die with Christ were not present for His burial! The grief stricken women who had stood near the cross followed His body to the new tomb in the beautiful Garden nearby. They knew they could not stay long. His death had been shortly before sundown, which signaled the beginning of the Passover Sabbath. Passover must be celebrated without the polluting influence of death. But it was important that they learn the place of His burial so that after the Sabbath they could return and continue the Jewish custom of anointing the shrouded body with fragrant spices.

His enemies soon learned the unwelcome news. The body of Jesus was now in the care of His followers! Something drastic needed to be done. They had to prevent Jesus' followers from manipulating that burial to make it appear that Christ had indeed risen as He had said He would!

How strange it was that even after burial, He was considered a threat to the political powers of His day. Again, Pilate was approached, this time by the enemies of

Jesus who wanted to assure that no one could steal the body and claim He had risen from the dead. This was just another in the series of unusual stories Pilate had heard about this mysterious Man who spoke of a secret kingdom. Pilate had a persistent uneasiness about the reality of that kingdom and the Man who wore a crown of thorns with a dignity he had rarely encountered. There was a peace beyond the power of Rome that had sustained the Man during the harsh trial, his scourging with the Roman lash, and the long last walk to the place of His crucifixion. It was reported that He talked to His Father during the agony of the cross. Who really was the Man who wore the crown of thorns?

The enemies of Christ appealed to the power of Rome to protect their interests by officially sealing the tomb and supplying guards to guarantee the seal. Pilate's answer was simply, "You have a guard; go your way, make it as secure as you know how" (Matt. 27:65).

Guards marched down the serene path of this third Garden in the Trilogy. The seal authorized by Caesar's representative was placed on the Garden tomb to guarantee the certainty of Christ's imprisonment in death. Stern-faced soldiers stood guard. Even in the darkness the message was unmistakably clear: "Rome is still in charge! Keep Out!"

One of the great enigmas of the resurrection story is why the enemies of Christ clearly remembered His promise to rise again on the third day, and yet His own followers, in the midst of their grief, failed to remember it, though He had repeated it so often. Perhaps the extremity of the taunting words and terrifying pain involved in His death had numbed them. It was a shattering experience to see two of the most trusted among the twelve fail: Judas, the group's treasurer, who betrayed Him for thirty pieces of silver, and Peter, who denied Him with cursing in the house of the high priest.

Was it at all possible on that fateful Friday for their tired, grieving minds to recall His words of the night before, as they sat with Him sharing a last supper together? He had made it clear that He would be betrayed by one of them, and denied by another. Yet after warning of these human failures, He had gone on to say: "Let not your heart be troubled; you believe in God, believe also in Me" (John 14:1). In that dark hour when it seemed there was no one they could still believe in, Jesus had encouraged them to believe in the God He had come to reveal.

Jesus understood well the darkness of grief which blots out the promises of God. Even He had cried, "Why have You forsaken Me?" But for the darkest hour, Jesus summarized the Gospel in its shortest form: the character of God never changes, and can always be trusted.

Those standing at the foot of the cross had heard His last words: "Father, 'into Your hands I commend my spirit' " (Luke 23:46). To the end He had known it was the character of God that was the Gospel. God's heart had always been the heart of Jesus' message. And the mysterious power of that Gospel had enabled two secret believers to bravely claim the body of Christ. It had enabled the grief-stricken women to follow His body to the grave. And it would enable the disciples who forsook Him to turn to Him again for cleansing and forgiveness.

Questions and mysteries hovered in the still morning air of the third Garden before the first rays of sunlight danced forth. The silence sheltering the sealed tomb suddenly shook with the force of an earthquake. The seal set by Rome to guarantee that Christ would remain imprisoned in His tomb was shredded by the touch of the Creator.

Early on the first day of the week a weeping woman stood alone outside the tomb. Through her tears she saw the huge stone had been rolled away. The tomb was empty! "They have taken away my Lord, and I do not know where they have laid Him" (John 20:13). As she cried out these words she turned around and saw someone.

She thought, *He must be the gardener!*

She said to Him: "Sir, if you have carried Him away, tell me where you have laid Him, and I will take Him away" (John 20:15).

The "gardener" turned and spoke one word to her. He called her by name: "Mary."

With joy she realized her Lord was the *redeeming Gardener*. At the cost of the cross, He had personally dealt with the thorns.

All questions find their answers in Him!

Questions:

Who really was the Man who wore the Crown of Thorns? How many people recognized Jesus for who He really was?

How closely had Christ identified with creation in:
  (a) His birth?
  (b) His stories?
  (c) His claims?
  (d) His lifestyle?
  (e) His death?
  (f) His resurrection?

Why had the women joined in the strange funeral procession from the Cross to the Garden Tomb? When did they return? Why?

Why had the enemies of Christ demanded guards at the sealed tomb? Why had the enemies remembered His promise to rise again when Christ's disciples seemed to forget?

Why did Mary Magdalene think the Risen Lord was the Gardener?

Chapter Eleven

———— • ————

News That Must Be Shared

———— • ————

*But the angel. . . . said to the women: "Do
not be afraid . . .He is risen . . ."*
—Matthew 28:5–6

Jesus met them and said: "Go and tell."
—Matthew 28:10

The role of women in the Garden story—and indeed
in the Gospel story as a whole—is often minimized.
Their participation in the ministry of Christ was much
less obvious than the disciples' public ministry. Because
their ministry was often hidden, we are in danger of
forgetting their contribution to the spread of the Gospel.

Again and again throughout His life, Jesus repeated
a basic theme of the Sermon on the Mount: the
importance to God of that which is hidden in our

lives—prayer, unselfish giving, and personal discipline. He affirmed God's appreciation of the hidden ministry of the individual person more than the ministry which seeks acclaim in publicity! In our publicity-driven society, this is hard to understand. Faithful women believed His message, and quietly, unselfishly witnessed by the power of their lives to the power of the Gospel.

Many of these women had followed Christ from Galilee. His last stressful days in Jerusalem were terrible to endure. The women who were with Him determined they would serve Him to the end. They were stunned by the cruelty of His death. Some of these women stood right at the foot of the cross with Mary, His mother, and with John, the faithful disciple Jesus loved. More women stood a little further away from the cross. They stared at the unspeakable horrors of the Savior's suffering.

The well-known disciples who had talked so bravely had forsaken Him. And unknown disciples had come forward to bury Him. In a terrible new loneliness these women realized how impossible it was to know what was hidden in another human heart. As the Master had so often affirmed, only God knows the secrets of the heart.

One of the women who followed Jesus was Mary Magdalene. Initially we are introduced to her during the early ministry of the Great Storyteller, while He was travelling through the towns and cities of Galilee. This was a time when society generally described a woman as "daughter," "wife," "sister," or "mother." Mary Magdalene bore no such customary introduction.

Only a stark commentary sums up the background of her life: "Mary Magdalene, out of whom He had cast seven demons" (Mark 16:9). The Cleansing Christ had completely renewed the meaning of life for Mary. In such wondrous newness, Mary became one of the group of Galilean women who ministered to Christ. (Interestingly, the word "minister" referred to in Matthew has quite a similar meaning to the Hebrew word "helper" describing Eve in the Garden of Beginnings.) Among that group of women were Joanna, the wife of Herod's steward, and Susannah. These women were sufficiently affluent to provide for Jesus out of their own resources. They supported the spread of the Gospel with the witness of their lives as well as with their money.

As His ministry touched and blessed more people, opposition to it also grew, yet Mary Magdalene was among the women who continued their faithful service as His followers. She stood near the cross. She was one of the small group who followed the strange burial procession, with the other women, to observe His tomb in the heart of a beautiful Garden. And she determined she would return, after the Sabbath, bringing precious spices. The Cleansing Christ was worth her very best.

So, on the first Easter day, "while it was still dark," Mary returned (John 20:1). Finding the open tomb empty, she was filled with fearful grief. Then through the blurred vision of her tears, she saw the Risen

Christ—as the Gardener. Was He enjoying the beauty and fragrance of the flowers in the light of the New Creation? Only when He called her by her own name, "Mary," was she able to recognize the Risen Christ and call Him by His own name, "Master."

Each Garden in the Trilogy is a special setting for the divine dialogue. The Creator seeks an understanding response from the persons He made in His own image. In Eden, His four questions to Adam and Eve were related to their understanding of their willful misuse of creation.

In Gethsemane the Great Questioner asked both His friends and His enemies to explain their actions: "Why do you sleep?" (Luke 22:46) "Friend, why have you come?" (Matt. 26:50) "Are you betraying the Son of Man with a kiss?" (Luke 22:48) "Have you come out, as against a robber, with swords and clubs?" (Luke 22:52).

In the Garden of the Resurrection, the Great Questioner came to a lonely, weeping woman and asked about her grief and her goal: "Why are you weeping? Whom do you seek?" Then He asked her to be His messenger to take the news of His Resurrection to his disciples (John 20:15, 17).

The Risen Redeemer understood her sorrow and the deepest needs of her heart. His respect for Mary as a person created in the image of God cleansed her attitude to herself, her neighbor, and her God. And His confidence in her as the first commissioned witness to the greatest event in history infused her life with meaning and dignity.

One of the greatest joys of the Easter message is that from the beginning, God used ordinary people to share His extraordinary news of the Resurrection. Christ sets ordinary lives aglow with His renewing power. Witness to the God who touches "common things of creation" is beautifully told in the story of the burning bush found in Exodus 3. Moses did not ask: "What kind of bush is that?" He knew that it was an ordinary bush, a little way from the beaten path in the desert. He wondered why an ordinary bush was not consumed by the fire. "I will now turn aside and see this great sight, why the bush does not burn" (Exodus 3:3). The God who sets ordinary bushes and ordinary people aglow by the fire of His Spirit calls ordinary people like Mary Magdalene to share the good news of the Resurrection.

The Tomb was visited again in that predawn darkness.

A small group of mourning women entered the Garden. These were the women who had come with Him from Galilee. They had stood by at the cross, and they had refused to leave the place of death until they knew what would become of His tortured body. With fear they had followed until they saw the tomb and how the body was laid. They planned to return as soon as possible after resting "on the Sabbath according to the commandment" (Luke 23:56).

The Sabbath was now passed.

See how quickly they moved in the darkness toward the tomb!

In their insecurity they kept so close to each other . . . as though they gathered strength by their closeness, sharing the Love that changed their lives. Their hands were full of fragrant spices, and their minds were filled with one tormenting question: "Who will roll away the stone from the door of the tomb for us?" (Mark 16:3).

There is no clear evidence that the women realized the stone had been authentically sealed (under the authority of Rome) with guards ordered to stand watch over the seal. This official sealing of the tomb had happened since the women had observed His simple burial. How would they ever deal with the weight of the stone and the power of the seal? Only under the threat of death could any person break the authorized seal of Rome!

But there was no need for human hands to touch the great seal. After a powerful earthquake, an angel of the Lord came to roll back the stone, and confidently sat upon it. At this sight the guards trembled with fear and became like dead men. But the angel said to the women: "Do not be afraid; for I know that you seek Jesus who was crucified. He is not here; for He has risen as He said. Come, see the place where the Lord lay . . . and go quickly and tell His disciples that He is risen from the dead . . . He is going before you into Galilee . . . there you will see Him." (Matt. 28:5-7).

Reassured by the angel of the certain joy of Christ's resurrection, the women accepted the invitation to see (i.e., observe) the empty place where His dead body lay. Then they were commissioned to go and tell His disciples that they would see (another Greek word used here which means to more extensively observe) Him in Galilee. With joy the group of women turned to leave the Garden, running to share the good news with the disciples as soon as possible.

And look who was standing there in the garden, to greet them.

The Risen Christ, Himself, greeted them!

His first word of salutation, "Hail"

This "Hail!" is the very same word of respectful greeting which the angel Gabriel used when he announced to Mary that she would bear the Son of God. It is also the same word used by the Roman soldiers when they clothed Christ in royal purple, placed a crown of thorns on His head, and bowed before Him with their mockery of great respect, sneering "Hail!"

Nothing more dramatically expresses Christ's affirmation of the worth and witness of women in the Kingdom of God than His greeting them so respectfully, and commissioning them in the Garden of the New Creation for the great work of being His personal witnesses.

Unlike Eden after man's rebellion against the will of God, with its foreboding message of pollution and death in the forbidden tree, at the heart of this Garden stands the Cleansing Christ, after His full obedience, with the joyous message of life in the New Creation. "But now Christ is risen from the dead, and has become the firstfruits of those who have fallen asleep. . . . For as in

Adam all die, even so also in Christ all shall be made alive. But each one in his own order. Christ the first-fruits" (1 Cor. 15:20-23).

With what joy these women left the Garden of the New Creation! They came as mourners of death. They left as messengers of life! Here is perhaps the greatest example of the central role of person-to-person witness, in the ongoing Kingdom of God. No one less than the Risen Christ had asked them to personally deliver to His disciples the message of His resurrection.

The mystery of the resurrection is beyond words. It is the most profound mystery in the world. The earthquake that broke the seal authorized by Rome to imprison the dead Christ, still shakes stubborn resistance to the power of the resurrection. Ever since that first Easter, around the world in many lands and languages, thousands of books have been written, attempting to express in human words the divine denouement of the mystery.

In 1930, the book *Who Moved the Stone* was written by Frank Morison, a lawyer, who had originally determined to prove the resurrection was nothing but a myth.[1] The more he studied all the evidence, the more Morison felt deeply compelled to witness to his own final conclusion after detailed, critical analysis of the evidence: "The third day He arose from the dead."[2]

Millions of searching minds have pondered the reality and meaning of the resurrection. Some years ago the British Broadcasting Company produced a series focused on the question: "What do you consider the most important single question in all human history?" The prominent British philosopher, C. E. M. Joad, submitted his question: "Did Jesus Christ rise from the dead?" Joad, a searching agnostic at the time, stated that if indeed Christ had risen from the dead, all other questions were secondary. Joad himself later became, a witness to faith in the Risen Christ. And in 1952, shortly before his death, Joad wrote his last, and perhaps his finest book: *The Recovery of Belief.*[3]

The reality of the resurrection continues to challenge millions of lives around the world. But it all began in the Garden of the New Creation, just outside Jerusalem, when the power of the Creator broke the seal and caused the great stone to be rolled away that the Risen Christ might come forth in the garden. His resurrection glory shed a mystical light everywhere. Like the soft light of the early dawn shimmering on each leaf and flower, the Light of the New Creation filled the whole Garden with unspeakable beauty.

The women were filled with awe as well as joy. Could this really be happening to them? As women? After His wondrous greeting the Risen Christ had asked them to be His personal messengers! He confirmed the message given to the women by the angels who now guarded the empty shroud in the deserted tomb: "Remember how He spoke to you, when He was still in Galilee, saying, 'The Son of Man must be delivered into the hands of sinful men, and be crucified, and the third day rise again' " (Luke 24:6-7). "He is risen, as He said. . . . He is going before you into Galilee; there you will see Him" (Matt. 28:6-7).

With His ever-compassionate understanding of human nature, Christ spoke to the women. Deeply moved, they worshiped Him in the glory of His resurrection. They knelt that they might worship Him for *Who He really was!* With overwhelming gladness and gratitude, they affirmed the reality of the resurrection. They held the feet of the Risen Christ, yet fear was such a real part of this whole experience.

Quietly, Jesus again said to the women, "Do not be afraid. Go and tell my brethren to go to Galilee, and there they will see Me" (Matt. 28:10). Significantly in this unfolding story, the Hebrew word *see*, as it relates to the disciples, denotes a more prolonged observance. They would meet Christ in the quiet peace of Galilee. There, together they would talk things over in unrushed beauty by the seashore where He had first called them to join Him in the great ministry of the gospel.

The resurrection had not changed His character. But His identity had been fully confirmed. The Garden of the New Creation affirmed God's Good News: *Life will be eternally renewed.* Like the view from the mount that Bacon described as the only place in a garden to gain a full perspective of the whole design, the Garden of the Resurrection provides the eternal view of the promised renewal of life.[4]

"Tell the vision to no one until the Son of Man is raised from the dead" (Matt. 17:9).

Those were the very words of Christ to people who had seen strange and wondrous events in His life. Without the Resurrection, the message of Christ is incomplete. The message from the Garden of the Resurrection validates the meaning of His birth . . . His life . . . His death . . . and His promise of redemption and renewal of life in the Garden Planet.

Now this news must be shared!

Questions:

In what way did women minister to Jesus and to others for Jesus during His lifetime, at the Cross, at the tomb, and in sharing the news of His resurrection? How had their hidden ministry illustrated Christ's call in the Sermon on the Mount to serve God without seeking publicity?

What made the stillness and the empty tomb so awesome? What question did the angel ask the women? What message were the women to take from this Garden?

Who met them as they left? What was the *amazing* greeting? What glorious task did the Risen Lord personally give to the women?

Why *must* this news be shared? (Note that during His lifetime Christ followed some of His miracles with the words: "Tell no man until the Son of Man be risen from the dead!") How did the Resurrection affirm who He really was, and His purpose on the Garden Planet?

Chapter Twelve

———— · ————

The Harvest of an Understanding Heart

———— · ————

But he who received seed on the good ground is he who hears the word and understands it, who indeed bears fruit and produces: some a hundredfold, some sixty, some thirty.
—Matthew 13:23

Therefore, get wisdom. And in all your getting, get understanding.
—Proverbs 4:7

How differently the disciples reacted to the news of the empty tomb in the Garden! Numbed by the indescribable horrors of the previous few days and their overwhelming sense of failure, the disciples found the message from the Garden of the New Creation unbelievable. The women had delivered the message, saying they had actually seen the Risen Christ and talked with Him! Then why had Peter and John found only silence when they rushed to that same Garden? Entering the tomb, they had carefully examined the shroud, shaped in its strange, empty form. But they saw no angels. They heard no message. The Risen Christ hadn't spoken or even appeared to them when they rushed to the Garden (see John 20).

And yet the women insisted He had appeared to them that same morning. They bore the quiet certainty of first-hand experience. And they brought the mysterious message that He would meet the disciples in Galilee.

The women readily admitted they had been terrified. Both the angels who guarded the tomb and Jesus Himself had told them: "Do not be afraid." Only the Risen Christ could have assured them of the certainty of His good news, and His assurance was glorious!

But how could the disciples possibly believe these reports? The injustice and inhumanity of His death had shaken them. Evil had darkened any sense of truth and reality.

In the midst of their bewilderment and shaken hopes, two of the disciples set out for Emmaus. As they walked, a Mysterious Stranger joined them. He listened as they poured out their despair:

But we were hoping that it was He who was going to redeem
Israel. . . . and certain women of our company, who arrived
at the tomb early, astonished us. When they did not find his
body, they came saying. . . He was alive. And certain of
those who were with us went to the tomb and found it just
as the women had said; but Him they did not see.

Luke 24:21-24

The Stranger listened attentively.

He later gave His amazing answer!

Continuing their conversation, the disciples referred
to "certain women of our company." The ease with
which they made the comment illustrated their full
acceptance of the women's part in the company of
those committed to Christ in the work of the Gospel.
This affirmation of women's participation in the early
church is especially interesting in these days when so
much controversy swirls around the role of women,
both inside and outside the church.

But the Great Storyteller had an encouraging message for all people—men and women—who feel insecure about their role and identity in doing ordinary
tasks. Our modern world glorifies work that is publicly
recognized and scorns the often hidden ministry of
necessary mundane chores. By washing the disciples'
feet, Jesus taught the security of the image of God
fulfilled in ordinary tasks.

Jesus reminded His followers that God had created
Man—male and female—in His own image, after His
likeness. He had come to restore the identity of both

men and women to the full image of the love of God. He wanted them to understand the meaning and potential of each individual redeemed in the image of God.

The original *imago deo* was distorted by rebellion against the Master Artist in the Garden of Beginnings. Somewhat like the great painting of *The Creation* in the Sistine Chapel, the passing years further darkened and diminished the brilliant outline of the original. Christ came that the *imago deo* might be restored in men and women.

Just a few days before His last visit to the Garden of Gethsemane, a small antagonistic group came to belittle the Great Storyteller before a crowd gathered in Jerusalem. Seeking to ensnare Him in the unpopular issue of Roman taxation, they asked:

"Is it lawful to pay taxes to Caesar, or not?"

Jesus requested a coin and responded, "Whose image and inscription is this?"

"Caesar's," was the reply.

"Render therefore to Caesar the things that are Caesar's, and to God the things that are God's" (Matt. 22:17-21).

Jesus' point was that when people see Caesar's image on a coin they recognize the responsibility that places on them. Jesus asked them if they recognized God's image in their own lives and the lives of others— and the responsibility of bearing His image.

They were silenced by His greater question. "When they had heard these words, they marveled, and left

Him and went their way" (Matt. 22:22). But those who stayed to follow Jesus were amazed by His power to renew God's image in damaged lives. His followers were glad and grateful.

There was a wonderful diversity of background among the women who followed Christ: Joanna, the wife of Herod's steward; the Syrophenician woman who sought deliverance for her daughter; Mary and Martha, the two affluent sisters from a respected family in Bethany; and the not-so-respected Samaritan woman at the well. The Gospel writers were not name-droppers, and even people of the most humble backgrounds were important in their narratives. In fact one of Jesus' longest recorded theological discussions was with the unnamed, but not highly respected woman at the well in Sychar (See John 4:1-42). Jesus' respectful manner toward her startled the Samaritan woman.

She had come to draw water from Jacob's well. When He asked her for a drink of water, she was surprised, given the prejudice generally felt for Samaritans. She asked, "How is it that You, being a Jew, ask a drink from me, a Samaritan woman?" (John 4:9)

Then He began to talk to her as though she mattered in the kingdom of God. He spoke about living water that would leave those who drank it ever-satisfied, and offered that water to her. He showed her that He knew the inner environment of her spirit, her unspoken needs, and the shambles she had made of her life. She was awed that He could see her hidden life so clearly, saying, "He told me all that I ever did" (John 4:39).

When the disciples returned to the well they were obviously critical of the woman. So she left her water jar and went into the nearby city, telling everyone she met, "Come see a Man who told me all things that I ever did. Could this be the Christ?" (John 4:29).

This strange confession and stranger question stirred the Samaritan city. In response to her witness, people wanted to hear Jesus for themselves. They invited Him to stay with them—Samaritans!—and He accepted their invitation. He stayed with them two days so they could hear first-hand the message of living water and the renewed image of God in the inner environment of the spirit. And they responded with faith: "Now we believe, not because of what you said, for we have heard for ourselves and know that this is indeed the Christ the Savior of the world" (John 4:42).

The message of living water and the renewed *imago deo* was indeed meant for the whole world.

Wherever He went, Christ recognized and affirmed the individual worth of each person. He demonstrated this in the home of Mary, Martha, and Lazarus of Bethany, where He appreciated the welcome of understanding hearts.

That home had often been a place of refreshing quiet during the demanding days of His ministry. During Jesus' visits, Mary took every possible opportunity to sit at His feet and learn the meaning of His life and her own, even though her sister Martha criticized her for not being practical.

Just a few days before His triumphal entry into Jerusalem, Jesus and His disciples were, once again, welcomed for a family meal. This was the last family supper He would share in their home before His death. While the disciples and Jesus were still visiting around the table, Mary brought an exquisite gift to Jesus: an alabaster flask of the most expensive ointment. Some scholars estimate the cost of this ointment to be the equivalent of a year's wages. It was the kind of extremely costly spikenard that could only be afforded for the burial of very wealthy people. To the disciples' amazement, Mary broke the beautiful flask and anointed Christ with the spikenard.

The fragrance filled the house—and indignation filled the disciples! Judas asked, "To what pupose is this waste? For this fragrant oil might have been sold for much and given to the poor" (Matt. 26:8–9).

But Jesus knew that Mary *understood* something of His life and mission. In her quiet meditation on His teachings, she perceived what His busy disciples could not see: the meaning of His imminent death. He spent much more time with his busy, "practical" disciples, but it was Mary who realized He was about to fulfill His promise to die for their redemption.

The exquisite fragrance of spikenard which filled the house at Bethany was mingled with Mary's "fragrance of His knowledge" (2 Cor. 2:14). Mary understood the meaning of the spikenard. In a few days the Passover would draw Jesus to Jerusalem, where He must face persecution and death. Now, while there was still time, she wanted to express her gratitude to the Cleansing Christ. She recognized the unique opportunity to do something beautiful for God.

The disciples were so critical of Mary that the Great Questioner asked them, "Why must you make this woman feel uncomfortable? She has done a beautiful thing for me.....When she poured this perfume on my body, she was preparing it for my burial. I assure you that wherever the Gospel is preached throughout the whole world, this deed of hers will also be recounted, as her memorial to me" (Matt. 26:10-12, Phillips). Mary's understanding of His death made her gift beautiful beyond words.

Understanding of the heart was treasured most by Jesus! This anointing for His death and burial revealed Mary's supreme gift of understanding. So few of those around Jesus seemed to know the real meaning of the proverb, "And in all your getting, get understanding"(Prov. 4:7). That was why, even after His death and resurrection, the Great Questioner asked His disciples on the Emmaus road: "Aren't you failing to understand, and slow to believe in all that the prophets have said?" (Luke 24:25, Phillips)

Earlier roadside conversations with Jesus had only revealed how little the disciples *understood* Jesus' teaching and the meaning of "greatness" in the Kingdom of God. The Gospels openly admit the disciples' very human feelings of anger, doubt, and selfishness. Jesus once asked them about an argument they had on the road to Jerusalem when they thought He was out of earshot (Mark 9:33-35). The chagrined disciples admitted a power struggle about who would be the greatest among them. Their conversation on the road had been a furious argument over who would be the greatest and have the most authority in the kingdom they anticipated. Greatness and authority are still thorny problems in the Garden Planet!

Again and again, Jesus described authority in the kingdom of God: *the opportunity to serve others.* To His skeptical disciples, He offered the example of His own life: "For even the Son of Man did not come to be served, but to serve, and to give His life a ransom for many" (Mark 10:45). Though in the world great men enforced the weight of their authority, Christ called His disciples to help others feel the lift of love.

If only they could *understand.*

Sometimes the Great Storyteller used parables to illustrate important points. He was a master at understanding people and relating to their interests. He drew pictures with words about their actual lives and innermost thoughts. His searching eyes and expressive voice were unforgettable.

One of the best known and most frequently quoted parables is about a sower of seed (Mark 4:1-20). Everyone could recognize the setting: the familiar local sight of a plainly-dressed man walking slowly across his land. With careful motions he removed a handful of seed which filled the large, well-worn pouch slung from his shoulder. The seed was precious; it must not be wasted. And not one cubit of the land must be left unseeded.

There were different kinds of soil on his land, but the task of the sower was to scatter the seed widely and wisely. The harvest would prove the real worth of the different kinds of soil. His listeners recognized the four kinds of soil: the foot-trampled path resistant to growth; the thin layer of soil that deceptively covered hard, hidden rock; the choked soil, too overcrowded by thorns to provide for the seed; and the rich soil, well prepared for good growth. Closing the parable, Jesus cried, "He who has ears to hear, let him hear!" (Mark 4:9).

But the disciples didn't understand. When they were alone with Him, they asked for an explanation of the parable. Before He explained it, Jesus spoke about the essential dimension of hearing and seeing beyond the surface. Much more was involved, He said, than mere sound to the ear or sight to the eye. One must *understand* what was heard and seen. (Matt. 13:23).

This same profound concept was emphasized in 1987 by a distinguished physicist, Philip Morrison. In a televised series, "The Ring of Truth," Professor Morrison and his wife, Phylis, taught that vision is so much more than opening and using our eyes. Morrison's illustrations emphasized that imagination, judgment, and understanding are required for us to comprehend what we "see." Our judgments are internal, and the processes are complex. Morrison's modern day words apply well to Christ's ancient concept:

> Visual judgments require internal processes. . . . what we perceive is more than the sense organs can directly tell. . . . What we learn is rarely a free gift, some effort of our own must enter the transaction. . . . It is up to you to decide whether the evidence in word or image has the ring of truth.[1]

Jesus repeatedly warned His listeners that it was only in hearing with the inner perception of the spirit that they would truly *understand* His simple stories. Listeners merely content to "see" and "hear" in a superficial way were like the hardened garden path whose surface resisted any growth. Instead, Jesus challenged His disciples to listen actively, with the inner ear of heart, mind, and spirit. In essence, He said, "Be careful how you hear. Avoid superficiality. Hear with *understanding!*"

Jesus went on to interpret the parable of the sower. The Son of Man was the owner of the land. He carried the precious seed of the word of God. Wherever He went He spread that seed. He walked through the land hand-delivering the word of God to people.

The different kinds of soil represented the differences in the hearts of those who heard His words. The hardened soil represented people who had no living interaction with the Word of God in their lives. "He does not understand it, so the Evil One comes and snatches it away." The thin soil which covered hard rock was a picture of the person who responds emotionally to the Word. "Yet he has not taken root;" he falls away quickly in the face of opposition. The thorns that thrive in the nourishing soil are the cares of this world which claim the time and priorities of self-interested people. The essential ingredient in the soil was faith to hear and understand the message of God. "He who received seed on the good ground is he who hears the word and *understands* it, who indeed bears fruit and produces: some a hundredfold, some sixty, some thirty."

Perhaps no other parable illustrates so dramatically the difference which the *understanding heart* brings to life—the difference between bounty and barrenness. The renewal of the *imago deo* offered by the Cleansing Christ transforms the inner environment. *Understanding* nourishes the climate of the heart's soil, and the harvest is bountiful. The fruitfulness God intended for the Garden Planet begins in the rich soil of the inner environment.

Questions:

How did Jesus use a Roman coin to answer a question about responsibility to Caesar (government) and responsibility to God? Today as we consider the call to care for the creation, what is our responsibility to "Caesar" and to our Creator?

What does it mean to bear the image of God today, in the way we care for creation?

Why is it so important to remember Jesus' definition of authority as the opportunity to serve others, not our own self-interest? How would this affect our attitude to the environment today?

What can we learn from the Parable of the Sower regarding:
- (a) the great diversity of soil in the inner environment?
- (b) the good purpose of the Sower?
- (c) the meaning of thorns?
- (d) the good quality of the Seed?
- (e) the essential ingredient for fruitful life?

What does it mean to "love God with all your mind" as we consider environmental problems? Why did Jesus emphasize the needed *understanding of the heart* if we would deal with thorns in the Garden Planet?

Chapter Thirteen

———— • ————

Prophecy Fulfilled:
The Disciples Believe

———— • ————

We will not find strength in ourselves to dedicate our lives with the completeness which is demanded; we must seek it in our prayers.

—William Temple[1]

Ever since the Garden of Eden, prophets have proclaimed the promise of a Redeemer. They proclaimed it, though they did not always understand it themselves. Only history could reveal the fullness of the Creator's plan to deliver creation from corruption and make all things new.

Like a view through a telescope, God's prophets offered a glimpse into the future of His promises as they would develop in the setting of history. Often God used the prophets to prepare people for the fulfillment of His promises.

The Christmas story illustrates the beauty of prophetic preparation. A few people understood the meaning of the Savior's birth in the light of God's developing plan in history. Filled by the Holy Spirit, Zacharias, the aged priest who was the father of John the Baptist, understood the events of his day—in the birth of Christ—as the fulfillment of prophecy:

> Blessed is the Lord God of Israel,
> For He has visited and redeemed His people,
> And has raised up a horn of salvation for us
> In the house of His servant David,
> As He spoke by the mouth of His holy prophets . . . .
> To perform the mercy promised to our fathers
> And to remember His holy covenant.
> Luke 1:68-70, 72

Tradition tells us that Mary was in the garden in the Galilean town of Nazareth when the angel Gabriel approached her with his holy message (Luke 1:28–37). The fullness of time had come and the promise of a Messiah would be fulfilled through her:

"Rejoice Highly, O favored one, the Lord is with you. . . . you will conceive in your womb and bring forth a Son, and shall call His name Jesus"(Luke 1:28–31).

Gabriel's awesome appearance and his strange words no doubt frightened the young virgin. As a devout Jewish believer she looked for the promised

Messiah. Trembling with a mixture of fear and faith she asked, "How can this be, since I do not know a man?" (Luke 1:34).

The angel answered, "The Holy Spirit will come upon you, and the power of the Highest will over-shadow you; therefore, also, that Holy One who is to be born will be called the Son of God" (Luke 1:35).

Mary believed him, asking no sign to affirm the angel's message. But she was given a sign, the kind of sign that every woman can appreciate. Her aged cousin Elizabeth, wife of Zacharias, was great with child. Mary would have the understanding companionship of another pregnant woman who had been touched by the power of God—Elizabeth, who was far beyond the age of childbearing. Every time Mary looked at her aging cousin's bulging body, she would be reminded of Gabriel's words when he announced Elizabeth's pregnancy: "For with God nothing will be impossible" (Luke 1:37).

Mary is a powerful example of the strength of the inner environment. She faced ridicule, misunderstanding, and slander from snickering people who gossiped about her morality. Joseph, her betrothed, would have ended his commitment to her had an angel not dissuaded him in a dream. Even Jesus, in the midst of His public ministry, was once interrupted by a heckler who implied he had been born of fornication.

The clue to Mary's strength is summed up in the phrase, Mary "kept all these things in her heart" (Luke 2:51). The Son she bore taught the importance of the inner environment, and that what you treasure in your heart is the key to your whole life. Mary had a rich inner life.

No matter how concerned about her uncertain future, Mary revealed in the Magnificat, her song of praise to God, that praise filled her heart as she found joy in the character of God:

> My soul magnifies the Lord,
> And my spirit has rejoiced in God my Savior.
> For He has regarded the lowly state of His maidservant,
> For behold, henceforth all generations will call me blessed.
> For He who is mighty has done great things for me,
> And holy is His name.
> And His mercy is on those who fear Him
> From generation to generation.
>
> Luke 1:46-50

In the oft-repeated Magnificat, Mary spoke of God's work in history. She praised Him for fulfilling His promise of a Redeemer. Surrounded by misunderstanding and cruel gossip, she was grateful for the affirming words of those few people who understood the faithfulness of God in the birth of Christ. Shepherds came to worship the Good Shepherd who would give His life for the sheep. They told her that a choir of angels had sung the *Gloria* to celebrate His birth. Wise men from the east traveled a great distance and informed Mary of the wondrous star that led them.

It was not at the manger in Bethlehem, but at the great Temple in Jerusalem that Mary heard the glorious

affirmation of the meaning of His birth. There the aged
Simeon and Anna worshiped God, praising Him for the
child who would bring salvation to the world. No star
in the sky, nor choir of angels was needed to guide Anna
and Simeon to the Christ child. Inspired by the Spirit
they approached the temple to worship, just as Joseph
and Mary were bringing the baby to be presented to
God in the Temple as the Law prescribed.

Simeon had long treasured the prophecies of the
Messiah in his heart. He longed to see the Christ, but
knew that his death was near. Taking the child in his
arms, he recognized Him as the Redeemer promised in
Eden. Now death, which had also begun in Eden, lost
its faceless fear in Simeon's heart. Salvation had come!
Simeon blessed God, saying:

> Lord, now You are letting Your servant depart in peace,
> According to Your word;
> For my eyes have seen Your salvation
> Which you have prepared before the face of all peoples,
> A light to bring revelation to the Gentiles,
> And the glory of Your people Israel.
> Luke 2:29-32

Joseph and Mary marveled at his words. Simeon
blessed them, warning them of the opposition that the
Messiah would face in the future. He said a sword
would pierce Mary's heart as well—perhaps the ultimate
expression of the warning to Eve in the Garden of
Beginnings. But this Child would illuminate the inner

environment of all mankind, coming "that the thoughts of many hearts may be revealed" (Luke 2:35).

Anna, too, recognized the Christ child, and responded with worship and praise. An eighty-four year old widow, she had long looked for the Messiah. Luke tells us that after she gave thanks to God for the child, she "spoke of Him to all those who looked for redemption in Jerusalem" (Luke 2:38). So it was, in the Christmas story, that an aging widow became the first messenger of the Savior's birth to many in Jerusalem. As Simeon and Anna prove, the message of Christmas is not just for children!

Isaiah gave Christ a prophetic name: "a Man of sorrows and acquainted with grief" (Is. 53:3). He faced tests in the wilderness, taunts from the crowds, false charges by enemies, and failures in friends. These were all a part of the meaning of His name. His disciples were fallible men. He called, accepted, and loved them as they were. He understood them better than they understood themselves. Even the night before He was betrayed, He said to them: "You are My friends" (John 15:14).

The New Testament never portrays Jesus' followers as perfect people. Their weaknesses are painfully evident in the Gospels. When the Savior asked them to pray with Him in the Garden of Gethsemane, they fell asleep. Frightened by the horrors of His suffering and death, they deserted Him and fled. When the women told them of the Risen Christ, they doubted.

There were earlier indications in the disciples lives' that hinted at their vulnerability to such devastating defeat. The supper they shared with Christ in the upper room is a good illustration of their hidden weaknesses. Jesus had warned them on a number of occasions of their lack of faith in Him and their over-confidence in themselves. At the Passover table, He instituted the New Covenant with bread and wine, perhaps the most profound moment of His ministry on earth. Here the Eternal Ecologist outlined the remedy for the polluting sin of self-interest.

But almost immediately following the cup of the New Covenant, the apostles reverted to arguing about who would be the greatest. This self-centered conversation was a product of the same self-interest that spoiled Eden. In studying the life of Jesus, it is interesting to note that He continually called for followers, not leaders. He asked His disciples to see their primary identity as His followers—no matter how many people were following them. Even today, there is a stark contrast between the struggle for "turf" among those who see themselves primarily as leaders, and the search for "green pastures" among those who see themselves primarily as followers of the Good Shepherd. They are called to feed, not flout, the number of sheep in their flock!

So the drama of self-interest in Eden was replayed in the upper room. They simply did not understand the pollution of their own hearts and the costly answer He offered.

This blunt, unflattering description of the apostles bears little resemblance to their stained glass portraits in the great cathedrals of Christendom. The Gospels are clear about the depth of their doubt and despair after Calvary. Professor J.N.D. Anderson, Director of the Institute for Advanced Legal Studies at London University, pointed out the great significance of that despair.[2] In a lecture at Harvard University outlining evidences for the resurrection, he noted the great change in the disciples' attitudes. They felt despair, even to the point of desertion, before His death. Afterward, they came to complete commitment—to the point of gladly laying down their own lives for Him. All this was due to their utter certainty about the resurrection, and the tremendous change in them is an important part of the evidence for its reality.

Their transformation from despair to hope first started on the road to Emmaus (Luke 24:13–31). Perhaps to escape the stifling tension of Jerusalem, two of the disciples set out for the small community of Emmaus, some seven miles from the city. With the very human tendency to discuss again and again the details of a puzzling situation, they talked as they went about the crown of thorns, the cross, and the unexplained empty tomb. As they walked along, a Stranger joined them and asked, "What kind of conversation is this that you have with one another as you walk and are sad?"

(Luke 24:17). Amazed at His apparent ignorance of the events that everyone in Jerusalem was aware of, they reviewed the recent drama, and admitted their lost hopes in Christ: "We were hoping that it was He who was going to redeem Israel" (Luke 24:21).

They went on to tell Him of the astonishing report of the women who said that He was alive. But their doubts of the women's story were evident, for they added that when the disciples investigated the tomb, "Him they did not see" (Luke 24:24).

After listening to their own admissions of unbelief, the Great Questioner responded, "O foolish ones, and slow of heart to believe in all that the prophets have spoken!" (Luke 24:25).

It was then, on the road to Emmaus, that the Great Questioner framed with a question the mystery of the Garden Trilogy: "Ought not the Christ to have suffered these things and to enter into His glory?" And beginning with Moses and continuing through all the prophets, He explained to them all the things in the Scriptures concerning Himself. "And He opened their understanding that they might comprehend the Scriptures" (Luke 24:45).

The two disciples were deeply impressed with the Stranger. Describing the experience later, they said, "Did not our heart burn within us while He talked with us on the road, and while He opened the Scriptures to us?" (Luke 24:32) The cleansing of their inner environment had begun.

When they arrived at Emmaus, He accepted their cordial invitation to join them for supper. It was there, when He took bread into His scarred hands, broke it, and blessed it, that they finally recognized the Great Questioner for who He really was. But just as they recognized Him, He vanished from their sight.

All weariness left them as they hurriedly set out for Jerusalem to share the news with the depressed disciples. Even seven miles did not seem far in the face of news like that!

They finally reached the place where they knew the grieving disciples would be gathered. And they were not the only ones to report that they had seen the Risen Christ. "The Lord is risen indeed," they were told, "and has appeared to Simon!" (Luke 24:34).

We are told no more of that private meeting between Jesus and Simon Peter. The poignant beauty of that moment between the disciple who had wept bitterly over his denial, and the Risen Lord who had lovingly warned him of his weakness, is a secret wrapped in the silence belonging to the Great Storyteller.

As the roomful of disciples and followers puzzled over the strange reports that were coming in, Jesus Himself stood in their midst.

"Why are you troubled?" the Great Questioner asked them. "And why do doubts arise in your hearts? Behold My hands and My feet, that it is I Myself. Handle Me and see" (Luke 24:38-39).

Thus it was that late in the evening of that first Easter, the Risen Christ answered the questions that crowded their hearts and minds. The Great Storyteller said to them:

> These are the words which I spoke to you while I was still with you, that all things must be fulfilled which were written in the Law of Moses and the Prophets and the Psalms concerning Me.
>
> Luke 24:44

Then He opened their understanding to the great story of the Eternal Ecologist who had to deal with the pollution that could destroy the whole creation. He would deal with it from the inside out, from the causal condition of sinful self-interest in the inner environment of the heart. The message of the Cleansing Christ and the New Creation would be shared around the whole world. Eventually renewal would be complete in the New Heaven and the New Earth.

He asked them to join Him in sharing the good news of redemption. They were to be witnesses of the Risen Christ to the whole Garden Planet.

They soon learned how impossible the task was. The very first person they tried to share the good news with refused to believe them. Thomas, one of their own company, scoffed at their story. He bluntly told them that he wondered how they could be so simple minded as to believe it. In essence, he said, *Not Me! Unless I see for myself the nail prints in His hands, and feel the actual scar tissue in His side, you're not going to hear me talk about believing* (see John 20:24–25).

Thomas was a very discouraging example of the effectiveness of their witness. He taught them, right away, the problem they faced. Not until Jesus personally appeared to Thomas eight days later did he finally confess, "My Lord and My God!" (John 20:28).

And the Great Questioner said, "Because you have seen Me you have believed" (John 20:29). Jesus affirmed that the most blessed people are not those whose faith is based on the evidence of their eyes, but rather on the *understanding* of the heart that is beyond the seeing of the eye.

Perhaps the early Christians were reminded of this encounter between doubting Thomas and the Risen Christ when they read Paul's letter to the Ephesians praying, "the eyes of your understanding being enlightened; that you may know. . . His power toward us who believe" (Eph. 1:18-19).

There is no evidence that Christ added new teaching when He met His disciples in Galilee after the resurrection. But He did add the joy of understanding all that He had told them before the Garden of Gethsemane. The resurrection had not changed His story. The resurrection confirmed His story and His character.

He met with them one last time before His ascension from the Mount of Olives, in a simple gathering at the sea shore back where it all began. Early one morning the Risen Christ built a fire near the water's edge. The disciples had been fishing all night and caught nothing. As they approached the shore a Man called to them to cast their nets once more close to their boat. In response to His command, they made an astonishing catch. He invited them to bring some of the fish to shore and enjoy a meal over the welcoming fire.

After this wonderful outdoor breakfast, the Great Questioner had one last question.

"Do you love Me?" (John 21:15).

He reminded them that not blind faith, but only faith empowered by love is adequate to share His great story throughout the Garden Planet.

The love of God is the cleansing, creative power of the universe. Only those whose lives have been renewed and motivated by His redeeming love will understand His conservation program to rid the whole environment of polluting self-centeredness.

Witnesses to this redeeming love understand the words of Archbishop Temple: "Sin is anything less than the love of God."[3] They have accepted His call to become His co-workers in the redemptive care of His creation. His cleansing begins in the individual heart and extends to infinity. Those who are cleansed understand the Greatest Law of the Garden: "You shall love the Lord your God with all your heart, and with all your soul, and with all your strength, and with all your mind; and your neighbor as yourself" (Luke 10:27).

Questions:

What prophetic message of cleansing and redemption of creation was given in the Garden of Beginnings?

How did prophecy from Eden to Gethsemane prepare people for the fulfillment of the Creator's promises? What specific prophecies were fulfilled in the Christmas story and the Easter story?

How does the Virgin Mary's response to the coming of the Savior in her words and life illustrate the beauty and strength of the inner environment?

What changed the inner environment of the disciples from deep despair after the Crucifixion to joyous total commitment to Christ? How can you account for this change?

Chapter Fourteen

———— • ————

The New Creation

———— • ————

*Therefore, if anyone is in Christ, he is a
new creation; old things have passed away;
behold, all things have become new.*
—2 Corinthians 5:17

No doubt the new believers in the Risen Christ met
many people who scoffed at the reality of the promise,
"If anyone is in Christ, he is a new creation" (2 Cor.
5:17). Those might be easy words to say, but a skeptical
world waited and watched for proof.

The Cleansing Christ told His disciples how to
demonstrate the reality of the new life within them.
"Let your light so shine before men, that they may see
your good works and glorify your Father in Heaven"
(Matt. 5:16). Again and again the New Testament
reminded believers that lives renewed by the power of
Christ must bear the living fruit of love. "You will know
them by their fruits. . . . every good tree bears good

fruit," Jesus had emphasized (Matt. 7:16-17). The heart-deep ecology of the New Creation is known by its fruit of the Spirit: love, joy, peace, longsuffering, kindness, goodness, faithfulness, gentleness, and self-control (Gal. 5:22-23).

Since its inception, Christianity has brought the life-changing message of the love of God that causes good works to spring up; hospitals, clinics, orphanages, and food distribution are often visible signs of Christian influence. But the changes that the Gospel brings go much deeper.

We have a surprising source of firsthand observations on the transforming power of Christianity in the writings of Charles Darwin. Few people recognize that in later life Darwin actually supported Christian missions and wrote enthusiastically about the effects of the Gospel on native peoples.

Darwin was only twenty-two years old in 1831 when he was appointed the official Naturalist on the government ship *Beagle.* As he traveled to distant parts of the world, he carefully recorded fascinating observations about native people that he met. Visiting Tahiti in 1835, he wrote in his diary about Christianity's influences in changed lives, even bringing a new gentleness to the believers' faces. Charles Darwin's biographer, Peter Brent, relates:

> He filled page after page with details of their customs and fashions and of their reactions to their recent conversion to Christianity. Before sleeping on the open mountainside,

during his island excursions, he noted with approval and respect the prayers of his Tahitian companions. The missionaries, he felt, had done as much good as could be expected—human sacrifice, idolatry, war, and licentiousness had all been greatly reduced. . . . He seems to have seen [Christianity] as the arbiter and underwriter of the most important moral values.[1]

In a letter to his longtime friend J. S. Henslow, Darwin expanded his observations on Tahiti and its inhabitants:

Tahiti is a most charming spot. . . . Delicious scenery, climate, manners of the people are all in harmony. . . . It is moreover, admirable to behold what the missionaries both here and in New Zealand have effected. I firmly believe they are good men working for the sake of a good cause. I much suspect that those who have abused or sneered at the missionaries have generally been such as were not anxious to find the natives moral and intelligent beings.[2]

Darwin's commendation of the positive effect of Christianity on the Tahitian natives is more dramatic in light of his previous observations of natives of Tierra del Fuego. Visiting the country in 1834, he described the natives as "savages" who were "beyond the help of missionaries." He noted in his diary, "Viewing such men, one can hardly believe that they are fellow creatures placed in the same world."[3]

Admiral James Sullivan, also aboard the *Beagle*, debated with Darwin about the value of sending missionaries to Tierra del Fuego. He wrote, "Darwin has often expressed to me his conviction that it was utterly useless to send missionaries to such a set of savages as the Fuegian natives, probably the very lowest of the human race. I had always replied that I do not believe any human being existed too low to comprehend the simple message of the gospel of Christ."[4] But Darwin was eventually forced to change his mind, when he read about the tremendous progress missionaries had made among the Fuegian people. Almost forty years after his first visit to the Fuegians, he wrote Sullivan, acknowledging how completely he had isolated his life for scientific work: "Think what a benighted wretch I am, seeing no one and reading little in the newspapers . . . I had never heard a word of the success of the Tierra del Fuego Mission. It is most wonderful and shames me as I had prophesied utter failure." Impressed by the results of the work, Darwin annually sent financial support to the Mission. In the year before his death, he admitted, "The account of the Fuegians interested not only me, but all my family. It is truly wonderful what you have heard. . . about their honesty and their language. I certainly should have predicted that not all the missionaries in the world could have done what has been done."[5]

Darwin's comment about language is best appreciated by looking back to his diary on December 18, 1836. The use of words was completely unknown to the Fuegians when he first went ashore: "The chief spokesman was old. . . . He gave me three hard slaps on the breast and back at the same time making most curious noises. He then bared his breast for me to return the compliment, which being done, he seemed highly pleased." [6]

Darwin's written acknowledgment of the worth of Christian missions is rarely mentioned by those who quote his statements to support their scientific or philosophical views. Neither is it mentioned that in later editions of *The Origin of Species*, Darwin rephrased the concluding paragraph to include "by the Creator."[7]

The newness of life that Darwin observed in the Fuegian people has been described in various terms by those who know the Cleansing Christ: a new creation, born of the Spirit, and God's Garden.

The apostle Paul used a lovely garden phrase to address the church at Corinth. He described the community as a garden planted by God, and the apostles and disciples who brought the Gospel as laborers for the Great Gardener:

> We are simply God's agents in bringing you to the faith. Each of us performed the task which the Lord allotted to him. I planted the seed, and Apollos watered it; but God made it grow. Thus it is not just the gardeners with their planting and watering who count but God who makes it grow. Whether they plant or water they work as a team, though each will get his own pay for his own labor. We are God's fellow-workers, and you are God's garden.
>
> 1Cor. 3:5-9 NEB

Paul employed another beautiful image in his second letter to the community. In those days, some special gardens were carefully tended to yield precious aromatic spices treasured for their exquisite, lingering fragrance. Paul wrote of "the fragrance of the knowledge of Christ," which would have reminded the believers of the frankincense extracted from the flowers of many gardens and offered to God in worship; (2 Cor. 2:14-16, Phillips). Often the spices were kept and carried in a simple earthen vessel. Paul's words captured the image: "Thanks be to God who leads, wherever we are, on Christ's triumphant way and makes our knowledge of Him spread throughout the world like a lovely perfume!" (2 Cor.2:14, Phillips). He emphasized that Christ Himself gave the potency to this fragrance when he added, "This priceless treasure we hold, so to speak, in a common vessel—to show that the splendid power of it belongs to God and not to us."

Indeed the fragrant knowledge of the good news and the growing garden spread rapidly through the Roman world. Many responded to the story of the Cleansing Christ who wore the crown of thorns. The church, as the garden of God, sprang up like an oasis of the Spirit nurturing those who hungered and thirsted for God.

Again and again the Good Shepherd had reminded His followers they were to be concerned about creating an environment of green pastures for His sheep. He wanted the hungry of the world to be offered the Living Bread of the Gospel. Bishop T. D. Niles of India often described the sharing of the Gospel as "one beggar telling another beggar where to get the Bread of Life."

Jesus talked to His disciples about their literal responsibility to feed the hungry. Once, when crowds of people had come long distances to hear His message, and Jesus said, "I have compassion on the multitude, because they have now continued with Me three days and have nothing to eat. And I do not want to send them away hungry, lest they faint on the way" (Matt. 15:32). To the disciples amazement, Jesus told them they had a responsibility to meet the needs of all those hungry people!

He also taught them about their responsibility to meet the hidden hunger of people—the need to know the love of God in the inner environment of the spirit.

Peter, the rugged fisherman, had been among the disciples who watched Christ feed the multitudes. That memory was dim compared to the time the Risen Christ had prepared breakfast early one morning for a small group of hungry, tired disciples.

Peter often relived the story in his mind. It had been the turning point in his whole life. As he grew older he liked to share the story again when people told him they were tired or discouraged, or hungry for meaning in their life.

He remembered how tired and hungry and discouraged he was on that day. The sun was just beginning to outline the shape of the shore. The disciples had fished all night and caught nothing. Their boats were empty of fish; their hearts filled with failure. They knew the best fishing was before sunrise; already the pre-dawn glow was declaring the end of night. Tired, cold, and hungry, they could dimly see a solitary figure on the beach who told them to try again; and when they did, their nets were filled with fish!

Peter's memory of his own hunger and despair, and his sense of failure, often caused him to retell the story to those who spoke of despair in their own lives. In the dimness of that day, Peter had not been able to recognize the One who had called from the shore. But another disciple had understood. It was the Lord! Impetuously Peter jumped into the water to greet Him. Peter had first heard Christ's call to follow Him, long ago, by this very sea. But he had not followed faithfully, and had publicly denied Him with the salty curses that were a part of his life before he met the Great Questioner. What question would He ask now, by this same sea?

A glowing fire greeted the cold, hungry disciples.

Jesus, Himself, had built the fire.

He'd even cooked breakfast for them; hot bread and broiled fish were kept piping hot by the glowing coals.

"Come and eat breakfast" (John 21:12).

Jesus greeted them warmly. He took the bread and gave it to them, and so with the fish. Jesus knew what it was to be hungry.

Again and again, Peter encouraged others, who were depressed, with the story of that breakfast and the question Jesus asked. He never tired of repeating the question.

It was the most central question in the Garden Planet.

The Loving Creator asked Peter: "Do you love Me?" (John 21:17).

It was the qualifying question of discipleship.

Love is the essential requirement of the living soul!

In the Garden of Beginnings, "man became a living soul" when the Creator breathed into him the breath of God (Gen. 2:7). The breath of God, Himself: the Living Spirit of Pure Love. Nothing less would satisfy or sustain the living soul. Without love, thorns would kill life.

Warmed by the fire his forgiving Lord had built, Peter was issued his renewed call. Peter, who had denied Christ three times by the fire in the court of Caiaphas, was given three opportunities to affirm his commitment to Christ by this seaside fire. The renewed Peter said: "Lord, You know all things; You know that I love You" (John 21:17).

And the One who knows all hearts smiled back at Peter.

"Feed My sheep. . . . Follow Me" (John 21:17-19).

This call to care for others, in the love of Christ, was given again to the disciples when they gathered for final instructions on the Mount of Olives. His green pastures were meant for the whole world.

New churches spread throughout the known world. Inevitably, as their Loving Lord had warned them, with the growth of the Church would come opposition from those who resented its message of thorns and the need for renewal of life in Christ.

Fierce opposition came from the proud Saul.

One day the determined Saul was on his way to Damascus. He carried the listed names of those who preached the Cleansing Way of Christ. Saul's goal and determined commission was to have them killed. As he journeyed to Damascus, the Great Questioner confronted him by name:

"Saul, Saul why are you persecuting Me? . . . . It is hard for you to kick against the goads" (Acts 9:4-5).

The Greek word translated "goad" means something that pricks or stings—reminiscent of the thorns of Eden. It is so painful to acknowledge the reality of thorns!

"Who are You, Lord?" was Saul's frightened response.

"I am Jesus, whom you are persecuting" (Acts 9:5).

The blinding apparition plunged him into darkness. He agonized for three days until the Lord sent a faithful disciple to pray for him and restore his sight. As his eyes had been opened, he was sent to the Gentiles to fulfill the commission he had received on the Damascus road, to open the eyes of the people and to turn them from darkness to light.

The Risen Christ renewed the life of the proud, persecuting Saul. With a new name, Paul, and a renewed nature, he became a powerful witness to the world that "if anyone is in Christ, he is a new creation" (2 Cor. 5:17).

Paul wrote to many of the young churches about the meaning of creation and the promise of the New Creation in the Cleansing Christ. Early in his letter to the Romans, he spoke of God's magnificent message to all mankind, manifest in creation: "since the creation of the world His invisible attributes are clearly seen, being understood by the things that are made, even His eternal power and Godhead" (Rom. 1:19-20).

Creation, like an intricate puzzle, challenges us to find the hidden face of God in its elegant design. The invisible God reveals Himself in the world He made.

Immanuel Kant wrote, "Two things fill me with ever new and increasing admiration and awe—the starry heavens above and the moral law within."[8] These same thoughts are reflected in Paul's teaching about the witness of God in the great beauty of the environment around us and the great sensitivity of the environment within us.

Perhaps because of his love for God's creation, the apostle Paul also raged like an Old Testament prophet against the polluting power of evil. He declared that all have sinned and the whole world stands guilty before God (Rom. 3:23). And he did not shrink from acknowledging the influence of sin in his own life. He identified the needs of all mankind in the painful question: "It is an agonizing situation, and who on earth can set me free from the clutches of my own sinful nature?" (Rom. 7:24 Phillips).

From his own Damascus road experience Paul gave the answer: "I thank God there is a way out through Jesus Christ our Lord" (Rom. 7:25 Phillips).

Paul emphasized that the Gospel of cleansing, redeeming love relates to the whole creation in which God delights, as well as to mankind whom He created to share His joy. The New Heaven and New Earth is a central part of the Christian message:

> For the earnest expectation of the creation eagerly waits for the revealing of the sons of God. For the creation was subjected to futility, not willingly, but because of Him who subjected it in hope; because the creation itself also will be delivered from the bondage of corruption into the glorious liberty of the children of God. For we know that the whole creation groans and labors with birth pangs together until now. And not only they, but we also who have the firstfruits of the Spirit, even we ourselves groan within ourselves, eagerly waiting for the adoption, the redemption of our body. . . .
>
> For I am persuaded that neither death nor life, nor angels nor principalities nor powers, nor things present nor things to come, nor height nor depth, nor any other created thing, shall be able to separate us from the love of God which is in Christ Jesus our Lord.
>
> Romans 8:19-23, 38-39

The height, and length, and depth of all creation are encompassed by the message of the Gospel. The Lord who said "Gather up the fragments. . . so that nothing is lost" (John 6:12) will waste nothing of His creation, but will fulfill His purpose of redemption for us all. The

New Creation, a tantalizing promise for centuries, is being formed person by person, as the Redeeming Creator brings all of His Creation to its ultimate fulfillment.

Questions:

What is the basic life-changing message of the Gospel? Why is it important to remember that this good news of Renewal began in the heart of God, reaching out to redeem His creation even from the Garden of Beginnings?

What witness to the life-changing power of the Gospel did Charles Darwin make in his life-long observations? Throughout history millions have given personal witness to the life-changing power of the Gospel, people as different as: the former slave-trader, John Newton; the rich-born St. Francis of Assisi; the proud Pharisee, Saul of Tarsus; and the Albanian-born Mother Teresa. What message is central to their witness?

What amazes you most about the seaside campfire where the Risen Lord prepared breakfast for His hungry disciples and served them broiled fish and hot bread? What question did He ask Peter? Why is this the key question He asks all His disciples?
How does the apostle Paul relate the life-renewing power of God to the inner environment of the person,

and the environment of the planet as he deals with thorns in the Garden Planet?

Why does the apostle Paul call the church "the garden of God?"

Chapter Fifteen

———— • ————

Planet Protection in
the Greatest Law

———— • ————

*God so loved the world that He gave His
only begotten Son.*
—John 3:16

*Beloved, if God so loved us, we also ought
to love one another.*
—1 John 4:11

Echoes of the Garden of Beginnings linger in the
days, hours, and moments of history. There are echoes
of perfection, balance, beauty, and fellowship. And
there are echoes of selfishness, rebellion, and conflict.
The thorns of man's independence are scattered across
the valleys and meadows, the seashores and canyons
of time.

Christ the Redeemer, the imposing sculpture with arms outstretched in love, standing high above the city of Rio de Janeiro, was visible day and night from all points of the compass during the 1992 Earth Summit on the Environment. Even so the Risen Christ stands over all creation at the center of history. He embraces the gardens of the past and the future. He fulfills the hope of Eden, the prayers of Gethsemane, and the promise of the New Creation. He calls His followers to go forth in His Spirit to share in His work of renewing the environment of the inner person and the global planet.

But we must be realistic about today's mindset and recognize the problems we face in our own lives, and our whole culture.

The stylized motto of today's world could easily read, "I am the master of my fate." Madison Avenue sells the ethic of self-love and self-interest. The lifestyle of the luxurious gadget-filled home is a potent metaphor of our times. These lavish dwellings epitomize the values of money, pleasure, and status that are exalted in our society. Filled with the accelerated schedules of working parents, they are empty of unrushed happiness. Unloved or unappreciated children run away from home. Many of them commit suicide, never followed or found by caring parents. Unloving marriages die in divorce. Environmentally induced diseases bring a strange pallor to the faces of rich and poor alike around the world.

William Temple pinpoints the root cause of this night-marish existence: "There is only one sin, and it is characteristic of the whole world.   It is the self-will which prefers 'my way' to God's, which puts 'me' in the center where God is in place.   It pervades the universe."[1] When self takes first place, the inner environment shrivels and dies for lack of spiritual food and living water.

Water is, perhaps, the perfect example of what mankind has done to the Garden Planet. Throughout the world the water supply has become one of the greatest causes of disease, and every year the problem gets worse. Our once well-watered garden has been drained almost dry to meet the demands of our lavish lifestyle.   And while we drill deeper and deeper wells to satisfy our insatiable desires, we manage to pollute the purity of our remaining, though ever-diminishing supply.

People talk often about the problem of pollution. Their coffee-table books and magazines vividly describe the environmental crisis.   Nature calendars decorate their walls. Popular programs on pollution appear regularly on big-screen televisions. And they all prove interesting!

But such books, magazines, calendars and programs don't address the underlying cause of pollution or em- power people to fight it. Drought is not a problem of the physical environment alone. The Garden of the inner man can become parched and dry. Like wells that once held water, many hearts are now filled with dank silence.

These are days when people are reminded to be practical. The question is asked: "Is faith in God relevant to environmental issues?" Some speak of the Christian faith as "pie-in-the-sky-by-and-by." But those who have tasted Christ's living water for the inner environment know His present reality in the daily "here-and-now" of life. Today we need Christian stewardship nourished by meditations on the Creator's care.

I once heard a very eloquent woman proclaim tolerance as the greatest virtue in life. Challenging a dedicated environmentalist, she asked what emphasis on tolerance was taught by environmentalists: Could people decide for themselves what was toxic? With a kind firmness, the environmentalist replied, "Toleration of what causes pollution shows how little one is dedicated to the beauty and demanding rules of a clean environment. That applies to the whole Garden Planet as well as the inner garden of the person." Those two women debated long and had a lively discussion on the meaning of tolerance! No dedicated environmentalist sees moral worth in tolerating actions or attitudes that cause pollution.

Jesus came to shine a light on the hidden, polluted inner environment of mankind. The Great Storyteller, with piercing insight, drew His listeners into an examination of their own hearts. People whose inner environment was parched and dry listened eagerly to His stories, and His promise became real to many: "He who believes in Me, as the Scripture has said, out of his heart will flow rivers of living water" (John 7:38). Jesus' offered an inner resource that is like an artesian well of the Spirit springing up to cleanse and refresh, providing daily strength to those who walk in the Master Gardener's service.

Each individual must tap this power source directly. It is not something that one can understand secondhand, or receive from anyone except the Master Gardener Himself. In *Evidence for the Resurrection*, Sir J. N. D. Anderson underscores this point:

> The ultimate proof of the resurrection for each individual lies in his own knowledge of the risen Christ, for in this matter the evidence of experience can supplement that of history. Happily the promise of the risen Savior stills stands: 'Behold, I stand at the door and knock: if any man hear my voice, and open the door, I will come in to him, and will sup with him, and he with me' (Rev. 3:20).[2]

Christ still calls us to hear His voice and open the doors to our inner environment that He might enter our hearts and share His life with us. This was His call during His years of active ministry, as He labored to near exhaustion, preaching, teaching, healing, and feeding the hungry multitudes. The Garden of Gethsemane was a refuge for Him, a place to draw on His own artesian well of the Spirit, as He spent time alone in prayer with His Father. With that continual life-giving source of strength, He could face the demands that awaited Him. Like Adam, Jesus also struggled with the central choice of all history: to seek one's own will, or to embrace the will of the loving God. At the cost of His own life, Christ chose to wear the crown of thorns, that others might receive new life.

Unfortunately, many who have received Christ's gift of renewed life have failed to express their response in stewardship of the Garden Planet. The questions raised by Christian environmentalists at the Rio de Janeiro meetings seem more relevant than ever:

- What does the cleansing of man's inner environment mean to his responsibility for the physical environment of the Garden Planet?

- How should Christians respond to environmental pollution?

- Is the Church reminding its members that mankind was given responsibility in Eden to keep and preserve the garden?

- Where is the Church's voice on environmental issues?

- Where do we begin?

And the answer given at Rio becomes more fitting and meaningful in light of our inner cleansing: "Begin where you live!"

The starting place for planet renewal is not with *what you do,* but with *who you are.* Transformed inner lives should be marked by maturity, wisdom, and self-control. William C. Menninger, founder of the Menninger Clinic, developed an insightful list of the characteristics of an emotionally mature person:

> Having the ability to deal constructively with reality.
> Having the capacity to adapt to change.

Having a relative freedom from symptoms that are
produced by tensions and anxieties.

Having the capacity to find more satisfaction in giving
than receiving.

Having the capacity to relate to other people in a
consistent manner with mutual satisfaction and
helpfulness.

Having the capacity to sublimate, to direct one's
instinctive hostile energy into creative and constructive
outlets.

Having the capacity to love.[3]

What a meaningful description of concerned Christians, translating their inner peace and renewal into care for others and the world! They have faced the painful cost of thorns and asked the Cleansing Christ to forthrightly deal with them. And this cleansing shines out in their choices and lifestyle. They reject the driving, grasping pace of the luxurious living and the all-consuming career. Instead, these stewards of the Garden Planet model daily the Creator's care for His creation. Their lives are characterized by:

- a simple, caring, uncomplicated lifestyle

- an unselfish desire to share joy and purpose in life with whoever asks for help

- strength of mind to make and keep planet-preserving choices

- thoughtful "thorn-control" projects

- an ecology of life that encompasses both the inner and outer environments

- the amazing ability to turn polluted dumping grounds into gardens

- quiet walks to enjoy the beauty of creation and the blessings of the Creator in renewal of the spirit.

We can no longer afford to lose time. Our world cannot continue to focus on the immediate present and ignore the future. We cannot rely on another gallon of bottled water to solve our problems. There is a pressing need for commitment, but each person must decide for himself. After all, isn't that what Eden was all about? And for those who accept the Father's challenge to reclaim our world, the strength must flow from Him, as William Temple affirms:

> We human beings are selfish folk; and when we are tired we tend to be more selfish than ever. We will not find strength in ourselves to dedicate our lives with the completeness which is demanded; we must seek it in our prayers. This is a day of prayer and dedication; and our very prayer must be for the power to dedicate ourselves. We make it in the name of Him whose dedication was complete, "Who for the joy that was set before Him"—the joy of a world redeemed by Him from the misery of selfishness into the blessedness of love—"endured the Cross."[4]

Christians need a realistic understanding of the Gospel. We must embrace the good news that God will not allow what is evil and destructive to finally overcome the world He has created. The Eternal Ecologist desires to rid His world completely of all that pollutes, and He calls us to share that desire with Him.

The certainty of His ultimate victory is reflected in the inspired description of the sure, pure water in the New Heavens and the New Earth:

> And he showed me a pure river of water of life, clear as crystal, proceeding from the throne of God and of the Lamb. In the middle of its street, and on either side of the river was the tree of life, which bore twelve fruits, each tree yielding its fruit every month. And the leaves of the tree were for the healing of the nations. . . . let him who thirsts come. And whoever desires, let him take the water of life freely.
> Rev. 22:1-2, 17

One sunny morning, I meditated on the Creator's care for His creation, as I walked the island path to meet the mail boat.

Daily in the summer, come rain or shine, that ferry boat faithfully dropped the mailbag at the small dock about a mile away. As I walked across the meadow toward the dock, the ferry still wasn't in sight. I had time to pause at the head of the dock, and enjoy again the familiar, fading sign posted for so many years by the shore. Its message which had become a part of the private, welcoming landscape began: "In few corners of this mad world is it possible to maintain an area unspoiled by man's thoughtlessness." There followed the ten rules and customs that have held fast all this time, even though the message on the poster had been bleached by twenty years of sun. Just below the rules was the welcoming greeting with its unfading charm:

HELP US PRESERVE THE ISLAND'S BEAUTY

That fading poster seemed to me a parable. This ocean island, with all its quiet beauty, needed ten commandments on its guardian post. The island seemed a microcosm of Eden, with the rules needed to preserve its unique loveliness.

I laughed out loud at the thought.

But no one could hear that laughter, because the gulls flying overhead were loudly expressing their own laughter as they soared and wheeled in the island's wonderful freedom.

As I turned toward home, the quiet path led near the little cemetery nestled in the heart of the island. As with my first visit nearly thirty-five years before, I pondered the message on the stone that bore the name

ELIZA MOORE

Almost two hundred years ago, Eliza had come as a young bride to live on the ruggedly beautiful north shore of the island. William Moore had built a very simple home on the thirty-five acres of virgin land which directly faced Bear Island. From the path just in front of their home, Eliza could watch the splendid building of the bright, white Bear Island lighthouse.

One day good news came to William and Eliza Moore— they had been selected to be the keepers of the lighthouse. From that tall tower they could have soaring views of the wonders of creation, sky and sea, stars and stones, islands green with trees and mountains gold with sunset.

It was a demanding life. For many years they kept that light as the constant guard of a safe path through dark storms at sea. Eliza treasured her few uninterrupted hours for reading. At times she read aloud to savor the wonder of the words, especially when she read the family Bible, and thought about the meaning of life and death in God's creation.

As years passed, Eliza and her husband realized another move was ahead—to a place beyond the reach of the human body. They asked to be buried in the little cemetery near their first home on the island. Eliza remembered the days she had stood near that home watching across the water as builders checked the blueprints for the lighthouse. In the final move ahead, she looked forward to meeting the Master Builder of the Eternal Lighthouse, who had said, "Let not your heart be troubled. . . . in My Father's house are many mansions. . . . I go to prepare a place for you" (John 14:1–2).

Perhaps Eliza remembered words on another island, called Patmos, nearly two thousand years before. John, a disciple of the Master Builder, glimpsed the blueprints of eternity:

> The city had no need of the sun or of the moon to shine in it, for the glory of God illuminated it, and the Lamb is its light. And the nations of those who are saved shall walk in its light. . . . Its gates shall not be shut. . . .but there shall by no means enter it anything that defiles.
>
> Rev. 21:23-27

The sun added its glow to the happy line on Eliza's gravestone:

SHE SMILED IN DEATH TO MEET HER GOD.

That simple message—on a slender stone on a small island—celebrates the great joy of the New Creation.

Questions:

How does the world's diminishing supply of fresh water illustrate the growing environmental problems? What can we do to conserve water and protect its purity:
 (a) as individuals?
 (b) as communities?

Is the inner environment a starting place for planet renewal? Jesus spoke of the need for "living water." How is this need met? How does the renewal of the inner environment affect a person's attitude to our Creator and to all creation?

Do you believe there is a basic message Christians should share with others as we face today's ever-increasing environmental crisis? If so, what is the most effective way to do this? How would you express in your own words the message from the Gardens of the Bible?

How can meditations on the Creator's care change our lives?

References

Prologue

1. Donald B. Conroy, president of North American Conference on Religion and Ecology, spoken at Global Forum, Rio de Janeiro, 1992.

2. George Eliot, *Daniel Deronda*, (London: Chatto, Windus, 1922), 241.

Chapter One
Reflections in Stillness

1. Abraham Somes' Letters about Mount Desert and Sutton's Island, Archives of Boston Public Library, Archive file # G.41.60 (1916).

2. "From the Publisher," *Time*, 2 January 1989, 3.

3. George B. Dorr, Ernest Howe Forbush, and M. L. Fernald, "The Unique Island of Mount Desert," *National Geographic*, July 1914, 75.

4. Edward H. Cotton, *The Life of Charles W. Eliot* (Boston: Small, Maynard Co., 1926), 372.

5. Henry James, *Charles W. Eliot*, Volume II, (Boston: Houghton Mifflin, 1930), 206-7.

6. Sargent F. Collier, *The Triumph of George B. Dorr, Father of Arcadia National Park*. Privately published, 1964.

7. George E. Street, *Mount Desert, A History* (Boston: Houghton Mifflin, 1926), 286-7.

8. Dante, *The Divine Comedy, Paradiso,* canto 1, line 1; canto 33, line 145; canto 27, line 28.

9. Rachel Carson, *Silent Spring* (Boston: Houghton Mifflin, 1962).

10. "Silent Spring' judged influential," "National Briefs," The Boston Globe, 11 July 1992.

11. Eugene Mallove, "Do We Control the Universe's Fate?" "Outposts," *The Washington Post*, 30 November 1986, C3.

12. Freeman J. Dyson, *Infinite in All Directions* (New York: Harper and Row, 1988), 100.

13. Oswald Chambers, *My Utmost for His Highest* (New York: Dodd, Mead & Company, 1963) paraphrase of Psalm 139:9.

Chapter Two
The Ecology of Eden
1. Francis Bacon, *Essays of Gardens*, (1625), (Boston: Houghton Mifflin, 1936), 1.

2. Jürgen Moltmann, *God in Creation: A New Theology of Creation and the Spirit of God* (San Fransisco: Harper and Row, 1985), 4.

3. Saint Augustine, *Confessions,* transl by Henry Chadwick (Oxford: Oxford, 1991), 1.

Chapter Three
The Goal of Garden Relationships
1. U.S. Fish and Wildlife Service Report: January 1989.

2. James Fisher and Roger Tory Peterson, *The World of Birds* (Garden City, N.Y.: Doubleday, 1964), 267.

3. Dante, *The Divine Comedy, Paradiso,* canto 5, line 19.

4. *Ibid.* canto 3, line 85.

5. Jonathan Edwards, *Basic Writings* (New York: New American Library, 1903).

6. Esther (Edwards) Burr, *Esther Burr's Journal* (Washington: Woodward and Lothrop, 1903).

7. Plaque designed by Joshua Kendall's son William- text from *New England First Fruits*, 1643.

8. Edwards, *Basic Writings* (New York: New American Library Inc., 1966), 84-5.

9. Krister Sairsingh, "Jonathan Edwards and the Idea of Divine Glory: His Foundational Trinitarianism and its Ecclesial Import," Ph.D. thesis filed at Harvard University, 1986.

10. *Veritas Reconsidered.* Special Harvard 350th Anniversary Issue, volunteer publication of the Harvard Radcliffe Christian Fellowship, 1986, 19-21.

Chapter Four
The Tragedy of Broken Relationships
1. William Temple, Archbishop of Canterbury, *The Hope for a New World* (London: SCM Press, 1940), 14.

2. Karl Menninger, *Whatever Happened to Sin?* (New York: Hawthorn Books Inc., 1973).

3. Roger Lewin, "The Unmasking of Mitochondrial Eve," *Science*, 2 October, 1987, 24-26.

Chapter Five
The Sabbath Rest: Renewal for Man and Nature
1. George H. Williams, *Wilderness and Paradise in Christian Thought* (New York: Harper and Row, 1962).

2. Geroge H. Williams, "Christian Attitudes Toward Nature," *Christian Scholar's Review* 2 (1971) 1-2.

3. Carson, *Silent Spring,* 297

4. Jürgen Moltmann, *God in Creation* (New York: Harper and Row, 1985), 21.

5. Moltmann, *God in Creation,* 5.

6. Ibid., 6.

7. Ibid., 321.

8. Ibid., 246.

Chapter Six
The Renewal Offered
1. David Flusser, *Jesus* (New York: Herder and Herder, 1969), 18.

2. Timothy Ferris, "The Creation of the Universe," Public Broadcasting Service, November 1985.

3. Transcript, PTV Publications, P.O. Box 701, Kent, OH 44240.

4. A. H. McNeile, *The Gospel According to Matthew* (London: Macmillan, 1915), 87.

Chapter Seven
The Great Storyteller
1. C. S. Lewis, *Surprised by Joy* (New York: Harcourt, Brace & World, 1955), 236.

Chapter Nine
The Way to the Cross
1. Theodor Keim, *Jesus of Nazara*, Translated into English by Arthur Ransom, Volume VI (London: Williams and Norgate, 1883), 250.
2. Ibid., 250.

Chapter Eleven
News That Must Be Shared
1. Frank Morison, *Who Moved the Stone* (Downers Grove: Intervarsity Press, 1980).
2. Ibid., 192–193.
3. C. E. M. Joad, *The Recovery of Belief* (London: Faber & Faber, 1962).
4. Francis Bacon, *Essays, Of Gardens*, 1625. (Boston: Houghton Mifflin, 1936). 1

Chapter Twelve
The Harvest of an Understanding Heart
1. Philip and Phylis Morrison, *The Ring of Truth* (New York: Random House, 1987), 2, 7, 13. See also Public Broadcasting System videotapes, "The Ring of Truth," 1987.

Chapter Thirteen
Prophecy Fulfilled: The Disciples Believe
1. William Temple, *The Church Looks Forward* (London: MacMillan, 1944), 171.
2. J. N. D. Anderson, *Evidence for the Resurrection* (London: InterVarsity Press, 1969), 15.
3. Temple, *The Church Looks Forward*, 171.

Chapter Fourteen

The New Creation

1. Peter Brent, *A Man of Enlarged Curiosity* (New York: Harper and Row, 1981), 202.

2. Francis Darwin, ed. *Life and Letters of Charles Darwin, Volume III,* (London: Macmillan, 1887) Vol.1, 264.

3. Charles Darwin, *The Beagle Diary* (London: Macmillan, 1933), 212.

4. Francis Darwin ed. *Life and Letters of Charles Darwin*, Vol. 1, 308.

5. Ibid., Vol., 3 127–128.

6. Charles Darwin, *The Beagle Diary,* 119.

7. Charles Darwin, *The Origin of the Species* (Everyman's Library, 1963), 463.

8. Immanuel Kant, *Critique of Pure Reason* (1781), conclusion.

Chapter Fifteen

Planet Protection in the Greatest Law

1. William Temple, *Readings in St. John's Gospel,* (London Macmillan, 1937), 211.

2. J. N. D. Anderson, *The Evidence for the Resurrection,* (London Inter-Varsity Press, 1969), 16.

3. William C. Menninger, M.D., *The Criteria of Emotional Maturity* (Topeka, Kansas: Manninger Foundation not dated).

4. William Temple, *The Church Looks Forward* (London: Macmillan, 1944), 193.

Personal Meditation

———— • ————

Personal Meditation

———— • ————

Personal Meditation

———— • ————

Personal Meditation

Personal Meditation

Personal Meditation

Personal Meditation

———— • ————